The Guardian

QUICK CROSSWORDS ^{BOOK} 3

Published in 2022 by Welbeck
an imprint of Welbeck Non-Fiction,
part of Welbeck Publishing Group
Based in London and Sydney
www.welbeckpublishing.com

Editorial: Ben McConnell and Millie Acers
Design: Bauer Media and Eliana Holder

A CIP catalogue for this book is available from the British
Library.

ISBN: 978-1-80279-123-5

Printed in the United Kingdom

10 9 8 7 6 5 4 3 2 1

The Guardian

QUICK CROSSWORDS ^{BOOK} 3

A collection of more than **200**
engaging puzzles

WELBECK

About the Guardian

The *Guardian* has published honest and fearless journalism, free from commercial or political interference, since it was founded in 1821.

It now also publishes a huge variety of puzzles every day, both online and in print, covering many different types of crosswords, sudoku, general knowledge quizzes and more.

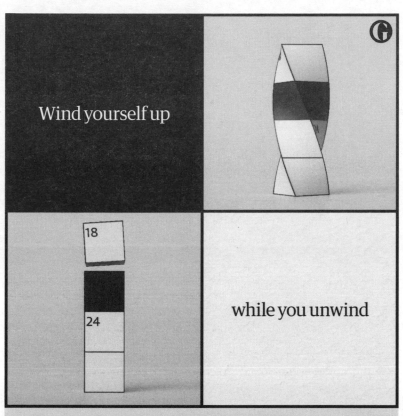

Introduction

Welcome to the third book in the *Guardian*'s challenging puzzle series. The humble quick crossword puzzle has appeared in the pages of the *Guardian* for decades, and these crosswords have been curated especially from recent issues to form a bumper batch of pure enjoyment.

These crosswords are designed to be solvable in a short time – there are not mountains of clues to work through. However, they are not easy. While a crossword expert may be able to solve them in a single break in the day, it is much more likely that you will have to step away and return to them later. Try it – your mind has a pleasantly surprising way of working on the answers without you even knowing.

Above all though, please enjoy this book! The world is full of challenges, but we hope that these challenges will provide a delightful diversion for you.

1

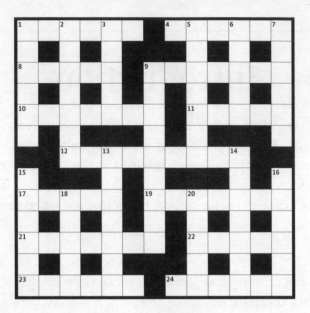

ACROSS

1 Verbal pedant (6)
4 Total — number (6)
8 Imaginary place for forgotten things (5)
9 Packing stuff (7)
10 Declare unfit for use (7)
11 Picturesque and peaceful scene (5)
12 Vanish (9)
17 Starting point (5)
19 Carve up (7)
21 When the sun is directly above the equator (7)
22 Propose for discussion (5)
23 Jumble (6)
24 Light-hearted (6)

DOWN

1 Plan of action (6)
2 Ron came (anag) — court (7)
3 Bit of rock (5)
5 Kind of wine or cake (7)
6 Make one (5)
7 Kind of electric switch (6)
9 Plant container on a sill (6,3)
13 Armoury (7)
14 Show off (7)
15 Not here (6)
16 Zephyr (6)
18 Turn down scornfully (5)
20 Add up (5)

Solution see page 233

2

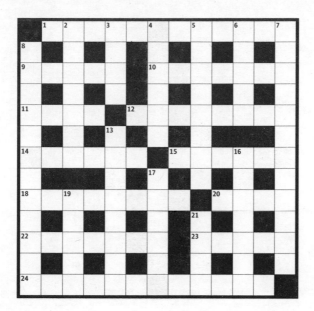

ACROSS

1 Person hoping to find sanctuary elsewhere (6,6)
9 Eliminating rounds of a race (5)
10 Nonplussed (2,1,4)
11 Collar — cop (4)
12 Spring-flowering woodland plant (8)
14 No matter whether (4,2)
15 South and Central American wildcat (6)
18 Not batting? (8)
20 Destruction (4)
22 In a state of serenity (2,5)
23 Prestige (5)
24 State of inability to manage (12)

DOWN

2 Disease (anag) — coast (7)
3 In case (4)
4 Ridiculously small (6)
5 Seen cave (anag) — disappear gradually (8)
6 Danish currency unit (5)
7 Determination (12)
8 Noisy but harmless pyrotechnic device (12)
13 Piece of unexpected good fortune (8)
16 Place of pilgrimage in the French Pyrenees (7)
17 Except when (6)
19 Discharge in disgrace (5)
21 Similar in character (4)

Solution see page 233

3

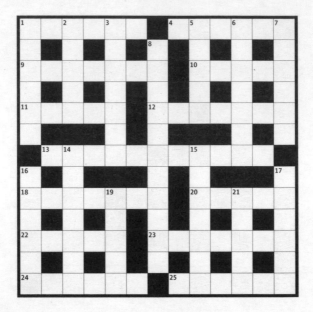

ACROSS

1 Burrowing marsupial (6)
4 Exclamation of disapproval (3-3)
9 Thing (7)
10 North African capital (5)
11 Thick woollen fabric from Scotland (5)
12 Low stuffed seat (7)
13 At all times (3,3,5)
18 City in Sicily (7)
20 Progeny (5)
22 Eggs on (5)
23 Spectacular sporting performance (7)
24 Conclusion (6)
25 Tickled (6)

DOWN

1 Abundance (6)
2 Bishop's hat (5)
3 Idealised pastoral setting (7)
5 Not censored (5)
6 Victory (7)
7 Causing difficulty (like a bed of roses?) (6)
8 Certain(ly) (6,5)
14 Accused, though without proof (7)
15 Corrosion-resistant metal, Ir (7)
16 Dapper (6)
17 Brought up (6)
19 Ascended (5)
21 Teams (5)

Solution see page 233

4

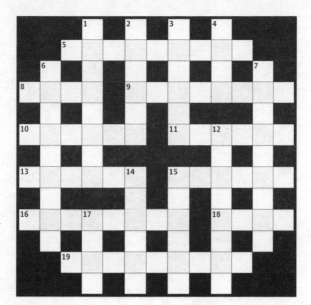

ACROSS

5 Cranky (9)
8 Device for moving liquid or gas (4)
9 Scottish broadsword (8)
10 Sports results — a large number (6)
11 Bewail (6)
13 Deep gorge (6)
15 Fit in (6)
16 London airport (8)
18 In that case ... (2,2)
19 Menial cop (anag) (9)

DOWN

1 Possessions, collectively (8)
2 Sign of the zodiac (6)
3 Humphrey Bogart's last wife, d. 2014 (6)
4 Strike violently (4)
6 Buyer (9)
7 Candour (9)
12 Unit of atmospheric pressure (8)
14 CS Lewis's imaginary land (6)
15 Archers (6)
17 Implement (4)

Solution see page 233

5

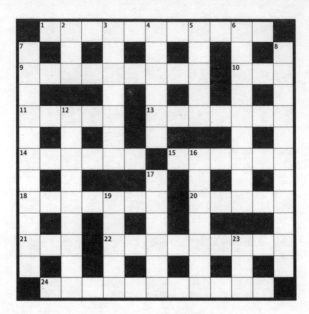

ACROSS

1 Fortune-teller's essential equipment? (7,4)
9 Haughty (9)
10 Greek letter T (3)
11 Dull and laborious routine (5)
13 Overbearing self-esteem (7)
14 Hidden — mysterious (6)
15 Alloy of tin and some lead (6)
18 Human body dissected by medical students (7)
20 Interior (5)
21 Chaps (3)
22 Hopeful people (9)
24 Mystic shape (anag) — branch of philosophy (11)

DOWN

2 Tear (3)
3 Fruit-filled pastry from Austria (7)
4 Instantly (2,4)
5 Washbowl (5)
6 'Humph', English jazz musician and broadcaster, d. 2008 (9)
7 The next world (7,4)
8 Newspapers engaging in sensational journalism (6,5)
12 Frequency (9)
16 Puzzles — riddles (7)
17 Support for a disabled person while walking (6)
19 Flower — stringed instrument (5)
23 (Of wine) dry (3)

Solution see page 234

6

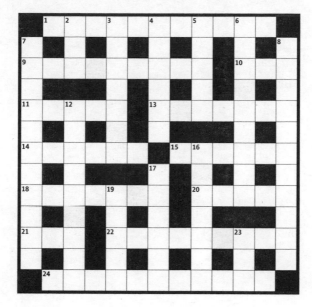

ACROSS

1 Boring tool (5,3,3)
9 Explain (9)
10 Hack (3)
11 Third letter of the Greek alphabet (5)
13 It's raised before the start of a play (7)
14 As a substitute (2,4)
15 Insect-catching network (6)
18 Nominal (7)
20 Gut-buster breakfast (3-2)
21 Expression of surprise (by a dove?) (3)
22 Globe vegetable? (9)
24 Old Maggie fan (11)

DOWN

2 Groove (3)
3 Bouquet (7)
4 Continent (6)
5 Put off (5)
6 Seriously ill (2,1,3,3)
7 Study of grammar, syntax and phonetics (11)
8 Young follower of latest fashion and pop music (5-6)
12 One of a set of 20 children have for starters (4,5)
16 Cop (7)
17 Poor unfortunate soul (6)
19 Lowest amount (5)
23 Elsewhere — unfashionable (3)

Solution see page 234

7

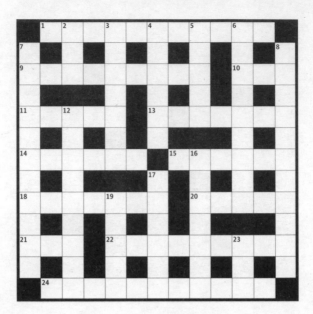

ACROSS

1 Extravaganza (11)
9 He starved (anag) — gathered food (9)
10 Bond (3)
11 Appearances (5)
13 Satirical drawing (7)
14 Make allowances for (6)
15 Weaken — sieve (6)
18 Much (7)
20 Before a given time (5)
21 Catch — after all deductions (3)
22 Innkeepers (9)
24 Reckoning (11)

DOWN

2 The norm (3)
3 Dairy products, can be hard or soft (7)
4 Hit out (6)
5 Below (5)
6 Armstrong or Sharman, say (9)
7 Calling into question (11)
8 Men's angle is (anag) — nonsensical (11)
12 Ensemble of players (9)
16 Sightseer (7)
17 Logo (6)
19 Theme (5)
23 In the past (3)

Solution see page 234

8

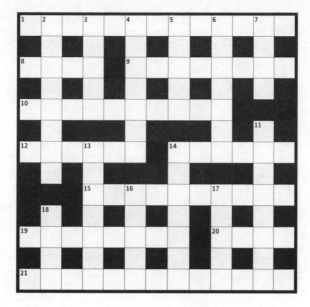

ACROSS

1 Thoughtful (13)
8 Adam and Eve's garden (4)
9 Each year (8)
10 Music hall song — scrap merchant's call (3,3,4)
12 Wrist guard used in archery — shot of Dutch courage (6)
14 Open-topped glass container (6)
15 Written missive intended for general consumption (4,6)
19 Cut of meat (4,4)
20 Neat (4)
21 Device for measuring radiation (6,7)

DOWN

2 Unexceptional (8)
3 Dance originally from Buenos Aires (5)
4 Follow a winding course (7)
5 Cruise ship (5)
6 Coach (7)
7 Field mouse (4)
11 Should it come to that (2,4,2)
13 Icebox (4,3)
14 West Indian ballad (7)
16 Old anaesthetic — three (anag) (5)
17 Giant — rocket (5)
18 Natural underground space (4)

Solution see page 234

9

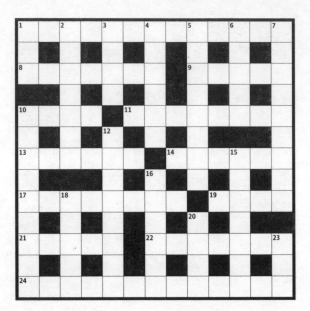

ACROSS

1 In a callous manner (4–9)
8 Wanting something to eat (7)
9 Two books of the Old Testament (5)
10 Most important aspect (4)
11 Where dishes are ordered separately, not from a set menu (1,2,5)
13 Run through (6)
14 Worn down (6)
17 Drug producing numbness and stupor (8)
19 Rope or wire used to support a mast (4)
21 Exhausted (3,2)
22 Glazed currant bun, often toasted (7)
24 Dancer is timid (anag) — treated differently (13)

DOWN

1 Police officer (informal) (3)
2 Lengthy reprimand (7)
3 Next in line (4)
4 For a short time (6)
5 Be cautious (4,4)
6 Railway carriage serving meals (5)
7 1965 Beatles hit (9)
10 Humbly asking (for a favour) (3,2,4)
12 Sailing vessel — sherry glass (8)
15 Diminish (7)
16 Short statement of a general principle (6)
18 Overturns — luxury car (5)
20 First light (4)
23 Termination (3)

Solution see page 235

10

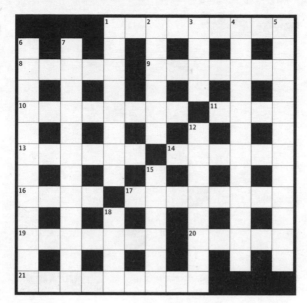

ACROSS

1 Late 1950s' genre combining R & B and gospel (4,5)
8 Thin cord (5)
9 Speak dramatically (7)
10 Space — role (8)
11 Reverse (4)
13 Contaminated (6)
14 Opening (of opportunity?) (6)
16 Carry (4)
17 Traditional Spanish lace scarf (8)
19 Acrid gas, NH₃ (7)
20 Training during term time for teachers in state schools (5)
21 Key (9)

DOWN

1 Initial investment (4,4)
2 Renew (6)
3 Treat with contempt — imitation (4)
4 Feature in decorative windows (7,5)
5 Period following the English Civil Wars (12)
6 Oscar knitted (anag) — what's necessary for carrying on a business (5-2-5)
7 Thick-skinned herbivorous animal of tropical Africa (12)
12 Invalid court procedure (8)
15 Wildlife-watching expedition (6)
18 In a little while (informal) (4)

Solution see page 235

11

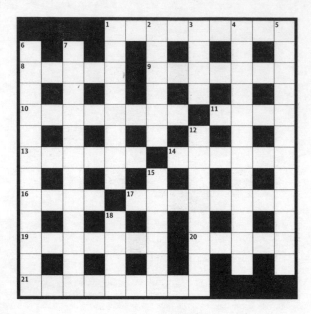

ACROSS

1 In flight (2,3,4)
8 Excite (5)
9 Betting adviser (7)
10 Railway service via the Channel Tunnel (8)
11 Animation (Italian) (4)
13 Whistleblower? (6)
14 Run headlong at high speed (6)
16 Listen to (4)
17 Brief pithy saying (8)
19 Scientist's protective clothing (abbr) (3,4)
20 Surplus to requirements (5)
21 Little plants (9)

DOWN

1 Supervised (8)
2 Venetian old master, d. 1575 (6)
3 Large international fair (4)
4 Lying between two extremes (12)
5 Celebrity chef, b. 1966 (6,6)
6 City in Los Angeles County, California (7,5)
7 Fit for matrimony (12)
12 Lady peer (8)
15 Absolutely correct (4,2)
18 Calm and collected (4)

Solution see page 235

12

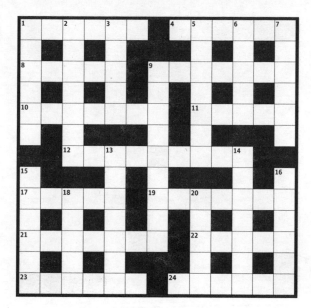

ACROSS

1 Combat (6)
4 Cows (6)
8 Type of type (5)
9 Employed (7)
10 Very last part (4,3)
11 Dire (5)
12 Using mocking irony (9)
17 Kilns for drying hops (5)
19 Surrendered (5,2)
21 1950s' popular music genre (7)
22 Search thoroughly (5)
23 Idle talk (6)
24 Baby's toy (6)

DOWN

1 Rebuke (6)
2 British soldiers (7)
3 Sudden forward thrust (5)
5 Side by side (7)
6 Robber (5)
7 Swamp completely (6)
9 Type of lens (4–5)
13 Soothing (7)
14 Cease functioning (informal) (4,3)
15 Mollycoddle (6)
16 Thinly scattered (6)
18 Quick (5)
20 Distant view (5)

Solution see page 235

13

ACROSS

1 Entreat humbly (10)
7 Brisk and lively tempo (7)
8 Coniferous tree with deciduous bright green needles (5)
10 Church in Scotland (4)
11 Besides (8)
13 Embraced (6)
15 Gretel's brother (6)
17 Plant used in perfumery (8)
18 Talented (4)
21 Use a divining rod (5)
22 Hurriedly (2,5)
23 Methodical (10)

DOWN

1 Powered by the sun (5)
2 Leaf of a book (4)
3 Watch without getting involved (4,2)
4 Dead end (3-2-3)
5 Prospers (7)
6 Flashy, cocksure young man (4,3,3)
9 Very rarely (6,4)
12 Enter, sir (anag) — put in again (8)
14 Yield (4,3)
16 Boredom (6)
19 Fundamental (5)
20 Informal conversation (4)

Solution see page 236

14

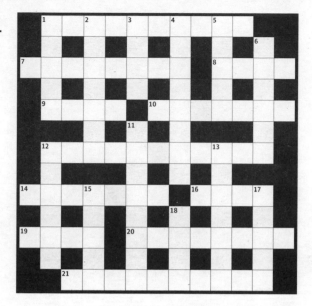

ACROSS

1 High-grade hard coal (10)
7 Compositions for orchestra and soloist(s) (8)
8 Still red inside (as hens' teeth?) (4)
9 Bean curd (4)
10 With enthusiasm (7)
12 Beautiful handwriting (11)
14 Fashionable hat (7)
16 Noddy's police constable (4)
19 Tiny brown songbird with a short upright tail (4)
20 Short competition between cars, requiring acceleration (4,4)
21 Person born shortly after WWII (4,6)

DOWN

1 In the air (5)
2 Showing sensitivity towards others (7)
3 Transport for vehicles with drivers (2-2)
4 Knightly behaviour? (8)
5 Austrian cake with cream, fruit or nuts (5)
6 Spoken (6)
11 Genius (8)
12 Age group (6)
13 One travelling to a sacred place (7)
15 Large bear from the bamboo forests of China and Tibet (5)
17 Interior colour scheme and furnishing (5)
18 Mexican tortilla dish (4)

Solution see page 236

15

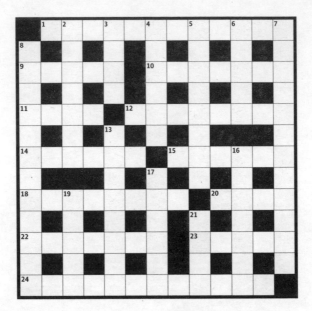

ACROSS

1 Snowdonia, for example (8,4)
9 Assume (5)
10 Unjust treatment (3,4)
11 Icelandic yoghurt (4)
12 Extremely lazy —
lie on bed (anag) (4-4)
14 Old Volkswagen (6)
15 Swing wildly (6)
18 Chosen (8)
20 That's funny! (2,2)
22 Fit (7)
23 Exclusive (5)
24 Childish verse (7,5)

DOWN

2 Bland and inoffensive (7)
3 Scrap (4)
4 Drug dealers (6)
5 Not intense (3-5)
6 Per person (1,4)
7 Orcas (6,6)
8 Resort city in the Basque
Country (3,9)
13 Obstruction (8)
16 Sports ground (7)
17 Distribute according to plan (6)
19 Failure (5)
21 Netting (4)

Solution see page 236

16

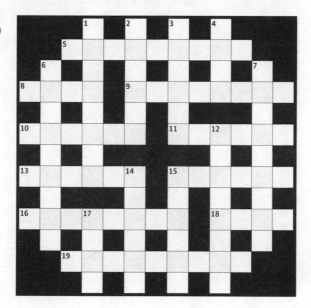

ACROSS

5 Golfing knickerbockers (4,5)
8 Strike — 1980s' pop group (4)
9 Term that is now fashionable (8)
10 High-ranking Ottoman official (6)
11 Make less (6)
13 OK, fine! (6)
15 Spectre (6)
16 Device for remembering things (8)
18 In this way (4)
19 Old gold coin (9)

DOWN

1 Low in calories (8)
2 Line connecting points of equal atmospheric pressure (6)
3 Heavy drinker (6)
4 Mixture (4)
6 Manacled workers (5,4)
7 Grumpy (9)
12 (At sea) deviation from the intended course (8)
14 Braying animal (6)
15 Classified (6)
17 Open to argument (4)

Solution see page 236

17

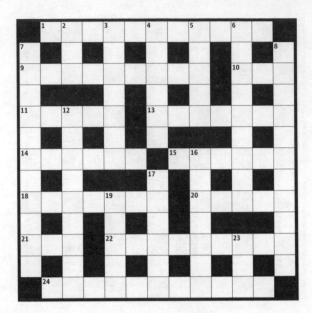

ACROSS

1 A word like 'before' or 'after' — pie portions (anag) (11)
9 Ardour (9)
10 Jazz instrument (abbr) (3)
11 English preacher and metaphysical poet, d. 1631 (5)
13 Gallant — in a hurry (7)
14 Find by searching (6)
15 Get free (6)
18 Batman, for example (7)
20 Last Greek letter (5)
21 Embrace (3)
22 Conserve made from oranges (9)
24 Large naval vessels (11)

DOWN

2 Oil-drilling platform (3)
3 Omen (7)
4 On an even keel (6)
5 Exams (5)
6 Stubborn (9)
7 Fingal's Cave composer, d. 1847 (11)
8 Overstated (11)
12 Largest Central American country (9)
16 Put up with (7)
17 Lack enough food (6)
19 Confess (5)
23 Unit of electric current (3)

Solution see page 237

18

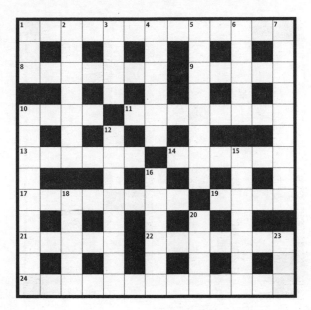

ACROSS

1 Doing nothing and hoping for the best — being Glenn etc (anag) (6,7)
8 Lockjaw (7)
9 Australian operatic soprano, d. 1931 (5)
10 Kind (4)
11 Punctuation mark (4,4)
13 Container used in lubricating machinery (6)
14 Lingerie — is nude (anag) (6)
17 Stand in (8)
19 Experts (4)
21 Nigerian currency unit (5)
22 Improving trend (7)
24 Scottish breed of cattle (8,5)

DOWN

1 Cricket club (3)
2 One regarded as sure to succeed in some field (7)
3 Departed (4)
4 Big meal (slang) (4-2)
5 Playing for stakes (8)
6 Brilliant success (5)
7 Austere monks taking a vow of silence (9)
10 Welsh national park (9)
12 Writer of light romantic fiction, Princess Diana's stepgrandmother, d. 2000 (8)
15 Moving slowly and carefully (7)
16 Accept as true without proof (6)
18 Elegance (5)
20 The Orient (4)
23 Hydrogen, for example (3)

Solution see page 237

19

ACROSS

1 Nearby game? (5,5)
7 Cause of irritation (7)
8 Deduce (5)
10 Light fawn colour (4)
11 German or Austrian motorway (8)
13 Bear-like (6)
15 Daylight robbery (informal) (3–3)
17 Leave behind (8)
18 Sleepy gape (4)
21 Given under oath (5)
22 Diminish (7)
23 Short movement between main parts of a symphony (10)

DOWN

1 Pilsner, for example (5)
2 Signals for action (4)
3 Hit hard (6)
4 Intermittent (8)
5 Animal whose milk made mozzarella initially (7)
6 Sycophantic (10)
9 Digit for the marital gold band (4,6)
12 Example (8)
14 (Inactive) industrial action? (3–4)
16 English actor, comedian and singer-songwriter (1915–2010) (6)
19 Television sound (5)
20 Catnap (4)

Solution see page 237

20

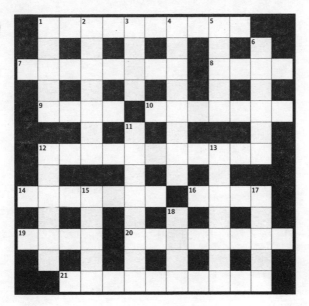

ACROSS

1 Complete (10)
7 Uninterrupted (8)
8 Wonky (4)
9 Promote (4)
10 Introduction (7)
12 Wrongly interpret —
I censor smut (anag) (11)
14 Give evidence (7)
16 Increases (4)
19 Let the cat out of the bag (4)
20 Hypocritical (3–5)
21 Parallel to the ground (10)

DOWN

1 Toady (5)
2 Greek goddess of divine
vengeance (7)
3 Addict (4)
4 Woman teacher (8)
5 Lag (5)
6 Active grievance (6)
11 It's thrown at newly-weds (8)
12 Breakfast dish (6)
13 Aglow (7)
15 Verboten (5)
17 Words used in a magical
incantation (5)
18 Non-starter (2–2)

Solution see page 237

21

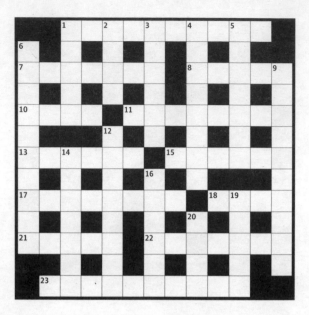

ACROSS

1 Inability to discharge one's debts as they come due (10)

7 Toiletry used on the head (4,3)

8 Mountainous state of western Austria (5)

10 Shed tears (4)

11 Secure position from which progress can be made (8)

13 Break in continuity (6)

15 Embellish with adornments (6)

17 Chafing — disharmony (8)

18 Fool — bird (4)

21 Pupil (5)

22 Most direct route (7)

23 Wear clothing typical of the opposite sex (5-5)

DOWN

1 Airship — barrage balloon (5)

2 Recess (4)

3 Trust (4,2)

4 Murphies (8)

5 Cause to rust (7)

6 Shoot the breeze? (4,3,3)

9 Philanderer (10)

12 Structure providing support (8)

14 Flyer (7)

16 Prohibit (6)

19 Single undivided wholes (5)

20 Selection of small dishes served in Greek or Turkish cuisine (4)

Solution see page 238

22

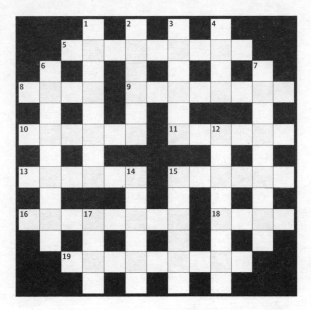

ACROSS

5 Policeman's club (9)
8 Suspended (4)
9 Ta-ta (6-2)
10 Spoken communication (6)
11 Settle comfortably (6)
13 Constantly (6)
15 Sea trip (6)
16 Sinister controller (8)
18 Reserve (4)
19 Fourfold (9)

DOWN

1 God heard (anag) — Irish port (8)
2 Informer (6)
3 Certain winner (4-2)
4 Deep feeling — music genre (4)
6 Adolescent infatuation (5,4)
7 Secret and illegal co-operation (9)
12 Bicker (8)
14 Fragments of metal, glass or rock (6)
15 In-crowd (6)
17 The sense you were born with! (4)

Solution see page 238

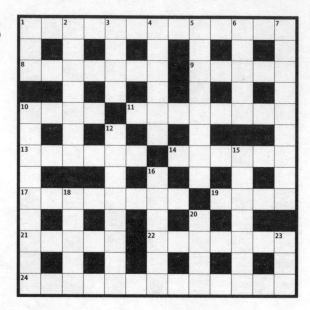

ACROSS

1 Informal expression (13)
8 Illegal game hunter (7)
9 A gastropod (5)
10 Aggressive youth movement of the 1970s (4)
11 Lacking shape (8)
13 Avian mimic (6)
14 Former pupil (6)
17 Working space for journalists dealing with current affairs (8)
19 Scottish hillside (4)
21 Follower of a major religion of the Indian subcontinent (5)
22 Rower (7)
24 Roadside greasy spoon (9,4)

DOWN

1 Surpass (3)
2 Student (7)
3 Honolulu's island (4)
4 Eradicate (6)
5 Collect in one place (8)
6 Spitting feathers (5)
7 Frothy mixed drink (9)
10 (Of food) likely to burn one's mouth (6,3)
12 Miserable so-and-so (8)
15 Deep toned percussion instrument (7)
16 With an ornately decorated style (6)
18 Dosh (informal) (5)
20 (Of some wine) very dry (4)
23 Born (3)

24

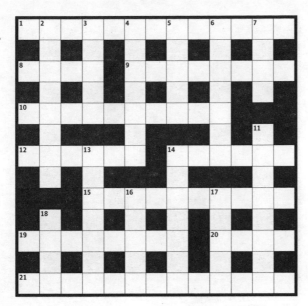

ACROSS

1 With little advance warning (2,5,6)
8 Finishes (could be loose or dead?) (4)
9 Weakness (8)
10 Philanthropic (10)
12 Financial plan (6)
14 Male parishioners (6)
15 Maize (6,4)
19 More than enough (slang) (8)
20 By mouth (4)
21 By accident (13)

DOWN

2 Inebriated (slang) (6,2)
3 Undue speed (5)
4 British soldier in the American War of Independence (7)
5 Aristocrat (5)
6 Writer of War and Peace, d. 1910 (7)
7 Astute — lovely (4)
11 Large room for drinking ale, typical of Munich (4,4)
13 Questioned intensely (7)
14 Handbill (7)
16 Robinson Crusoe's creator, d. 1731 (5)
17 Hit on the head (5)
18 Hold back (4)

Solution see page 238

25

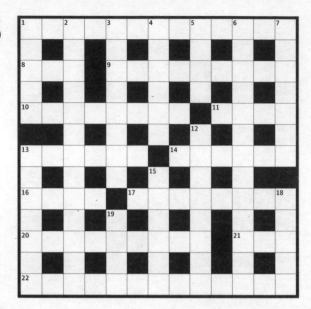

ACROSS

1 Drink made from West African beans (7,6)
8 Meadow (3)
9 Regardless of the price to pay (2,3,4)
10 Gob (informal) (8)
11 Roofed colonnade (4)
13 Blooming? (6)
14 Very nice (6)
16 Fizzy drink (4)
17 The 'x' in x3 (4,4)
20 Winter sporting device (9)
21 Pair (3)
22 Seek the impossible (3,3,3,4)

DOWN

1 Antiquity (5)
2 Striped stick from Lancashire (9,4)
3 Baldie (informal) (8)
4 Land for growing crops (6)
5 Kind of agate (4)
6 Immediately at the beginning (4,3,4,2)
7 River mouth (7)
12 Extremely inactive (4,4)
13 Pendulous-flowered shrub (7)
15 Gulf kingdom (6)
18 Prickle (5)
19 Longest river in Spain (4)

Solution see page 239

26

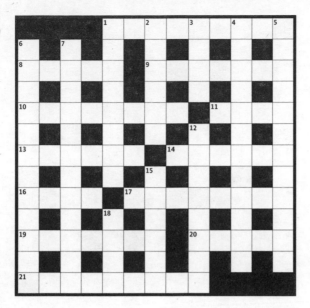

ACROSS

1 Below average (9)
8 Ms Winfrey? (5)
9 Words that are untrue or make no sense (7)
10 Fictional hero played in films by Christopher Reeve (8)
11 Isaac's eldest son (4)
13 Tap in a bunghole — GI's top (anag) (6)
14 As expected from the daughter or son (6)
16 Last Stuart monarch (4)
17 Asian shrub of the rose family — a cap join (anag) (8)
19 Coastal area between La Spezia in Italy and Cannes in France (7)
20 Greek island, capital Heraklion (5)
21 Heavy predatory mammal — evil owner (anag) (9)

DOWN

1 Fast movements in triple time (8)
2 University treasurer (6)
3 Heavy duty (4)
4 Begrudging (4-8)
5 Keir Starmer (0,6)
6 Small bird — rows up ashore (anag) (5,7)
7 A comic story? (7,5)
12 Person no longer hitched (8)
15 Strong-tasting green root used in Japanese cuisine (6)
18 Lake or pond (4)

Solution see page 239

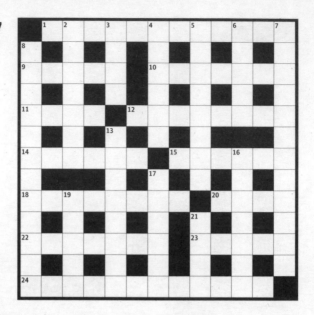

ACROSS

1 Almost impossible to comprehend (4-8)
9 Logo — pattern (5)
10 Shipment from A to B (7)
11 Deliberately have no contact with (4)
12 Finnish capital (8)
14 Largest city in Syria before the massive damage of the civil war (6)
15 Cherry brandy (6)
18 Republican's US rival (8)
20 Recognised leader in some field (4)
22 Admonish (7)
23 Short coat (5)
24 Swimming style (12)

DOWN

2 Stick one's nose in (7)
3 Pudding — useless — Homer Simpson's kind of beer (4)
4 Start (6)
5 Leather from nanny or billy? (8)
6 Author of The Master Builder, d. 1906 (5)
7 Kind of financial proposal with no realistic chance of success (3-4-5)
8 Style of robbery through a broken display window (5-3-4)
13 Deceptively pleasing (8)
16 Soviet satellite, launched 1957 (7)
17 Stroke gently (6)
19 Tree providing Canada's national emblem (5)
21 A night light? (4)

28

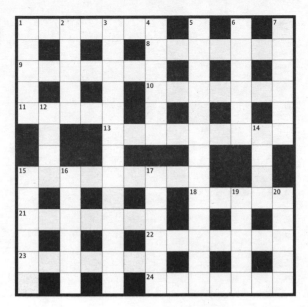

ACROSS

1 Heart-related (7)
8 Devotee (7)
9 English poet, Edith d. 1964 (7)
10 Direction in which the wind is blowing (7)
11 Clean by hard rubbing (5)
13 Elaborate (9)
15 Instrument measuring height above sea level (9)
18 Doughnut-shaped roll with hard crust (5)
21 Lady's chamber (7)
22 Egg white (7)
23 England's smallest county (7)
24 Voter (7)

DOWN

1 Expenditure (5)
2 Old-style (5)
3 Tall cold drinks — America's codes (anag) (3-5,5)
4 Telephone (4,2)
5 Always unruffled (13)
6 Naval force (6)
7 Crossing point (6)
12 Fashionable (informal) (4)
14 Accept (4)
15 Dark reddish-brown (6)
16 Dependable (6)
17 Protracted rant (6)
19 Full range (5)
20 Unsociable individual (5)

Solution see page 239

29

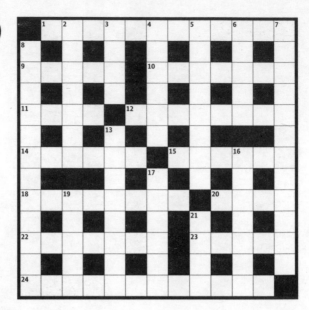

ACROSS

1 Recollected (6,2,4)
9 Supporting framework (5)
10 Put down (7)
11 Top of one's head (4)
12 Extra high male singing voice (8)
14 Inconstant (6)
15 Nibbles (6)
18 Front part of the brain (8)
20 Whimper (4)
22 Letters in sloping type (7)
23 Berkshire racecourse (5)
24 Neater column (anag) — terminology (12)

DOWN

2 Living in water (7)
3 Most recent (4)
4 To do with a fin on a fish (6)
5 Against (8)
6 Lifeless (5)
7 Very disappointed (12)
8 Extreme astonishment (12)
13 Vulgar (8)
16 14th-century English poet (7)
17 Edible shellfish (6)
19 Area of knowledge under discussion (5)
21 Small hard viral skin blemish (4)

Solution see page 240

30

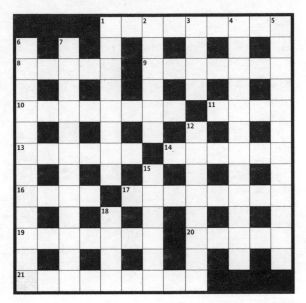

ACROSS

1 (In biology) series of changes in form that an organism undergoes (4,5)

8 Indian or Arctic? (5)

9 Admit (7)

10 Traitorous collaborator (8)

11 Partially carbonised vegetable matter saturated with water (4)

13 Second book of the Old Testament (6)

14 Pope's ambassador (6)

16 Grisly (4)

17 Paint with slight sheen (8)

19 Persuaded to join (5,2)

20 Spy (5)

21 Harvard, Yale and six other private universities (3,6)

DOWN

1 A floor covering (8)

2 Fertile (6)

3 Pious platitudes — jargon (4)

4 Trying too obviously to seem intelligent (6-6)

5 Coat thinly with a metal — let percolate (anag) (12)

6 Herbs in a small bag used in cooking (7,5)

7 Dictionary compilation (12)

12 Parasol (8)

15 Christmas drink (6)

18 Fringe (4)

Solution see page 240

31

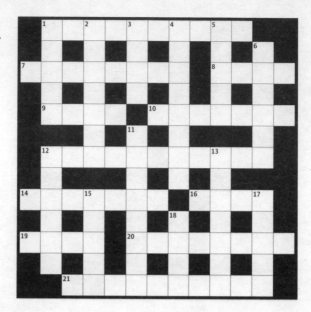

ACROSS

1 High-rise building (5,5)
7 Singling (anag) — a cocktail (3,5)
8 Pointed remark (4)
9 Price paid by traveller (4)
10 Laboured (7)
12 Penmanship (11)
14 Wealthy and privileged people (3,4)
16 Stare open-mouthed (4)
19 Mumble drunkenly (4)
20 Steadfast (8)
21 Bosses (10)

DOWN

1 He follows beggar man in rhyme (5)
2 Layabout (7)
3 Coot or moorhen, for example (4)
4 Flat-bottomed barges (8)
5 Faction (5)
6 Sinister (6)
11 Climbing plant — I re-saw it (anag) (8)
12 Hold tenderly (6)
13 Mollify (7)
15 Approximately (5)
17 Kind of programme — kind of light (5)
18 Stick together (4)

Solution see page 240

32

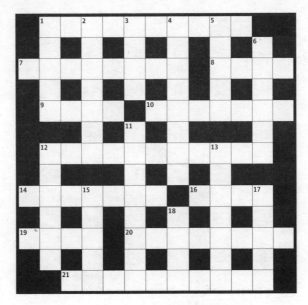

ACROSS

1 Regiment of the Household Cavalry (4,6)

7 Norwegian parliament (8)

8 Cosy corner (4)

9 Dilapidated building (4)

10 Legal pardon (7)

12 Where performers are congratulated by the audience (7,4)

14 Tailor-made (7)

16 Pleased (4)

19 Unpleasant child (4)

20 Hot spell (4,4)

21 African country founded in 2011 (5,5)

DOWN

1 By and by (5)

2 Horseshoer (7)

3 Grasp securely (4)

4 Altercation (8)

5 Reel, say (5)

6 Special website bringing together information from diverse sources in a uniform way (6)

11 Impertinent rejoinder (8)

12 Fruit with a stone (6)

13 Permitted (7)

15 Paved area next to a house (5)

17 English county (5)

18 Felines (4)

Solution see page 240

33

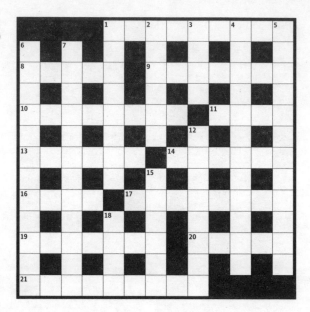

ACROSS

1 Properties of a space that determine how sound is transmitted (9)

8 Pull up (5)

9 Hot wind blowing from North Africa to southern Europe (7)

10 Like Janus? (3–5)

11 Having knowledge of (2,2)

13 Lamb or veal chop from behind the neck (6)

14 Work (6)

16 German car manufacturer, founded 1862 (4)

17 German motorway (8)

19 Slippery surface for recreation (3,4)

20 Fine net used in veils (5)

21 Make someone understand (3,6)

DOWN

1 Animal with long tongue that collects insects (8)

2 Thrown out (6)

3 Agricultural worker bound by the feudal system (4)

4 Miserable and beyond cheering up (12)

5 Fashionable upper-class young woman (6,6)

6 Anything happening? — hawking coots (anag) (5,7)

7 Old time corporal punishment (3,2,3,4)

12 Old time French dances (8)

15 Bird — bananas (6)

18 Thin plate (4)

Solution see page 241

34

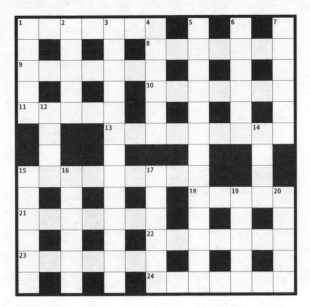

ACROSS

1 Oratorio on a sacred theme (7)
8 Pull out (of a race) (7)
9 Action to inflate one's sense of self-importance (7)
10 Made certain (7)
11 Ceasing to function (5)
13 Retire to bed (informal) (3,3,3)
15 Nonconformist (3,3,3)
18 Clips around the ear (5)
21 Italian dish (7)
22 Prince of Monaco, married to Grace Kelly, d. 2005 (7)
23 Liquorice flavouring — ie Danes (anag) (7)
24 Silk fabric (7)

DOWN

1 System of beliefs (5)
2 Girl's name — I moan (anag) (5)
3 Vertically (2,5,6)
4 Visual effect (6)
5 Sets of parallel lines providing shading in drawing (5-8)
6 Charts (anag) — formality (6)
7 Cheap and nasty (6)
12 Three feet (4)
14 Expression of incredulity (2,2)
15 Person involved with crude (6)
16 Condense (6)
17 Cook too much (6)
19 Pretend (5)
20 Middle Eastern country (5)

Solution see page 241

35

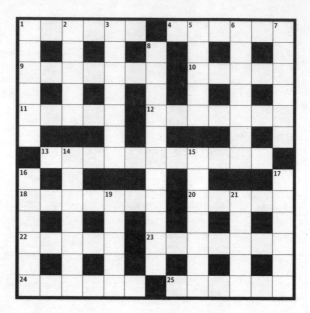

ACROSS

1 Withdraw (6)
4 Preparatory exercising (4-2)
9 With no exceptions (3,4)
10 Feeling of resentment (5)
11 Waive (5)
12 Bank employees (7)
13 Satisfaction (11)
18 Enclosed drain under road or railway track (7)
20 Out of sorts (5)
22 Bare (5)
23 Eight-sided figure (7)
24 Miscellaneous (6)
25 Worshipped (6)

DOWN

1 Cold-shoulder (6)
2 Person responsible for looking after another (5)
3 Cease to participate (4,3)
5 Horrify (5)
6 Fashion designer Alexander — film star Steve (7)
7 Give satisfaction (6)
8 Journey's end (11)
14 Waterproof cloth (7)
15 On horseback (7)
16 Fragrances (6)
17 Made amends (6)
19 Church official (5)
21 Plantation product (5)

Solution see page 241

36

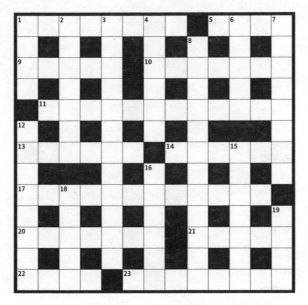

ACROSS

1 Thought out strategy (4,4)
5 Member of a people of eastern Europe and Asian Russia (4)
9 Garfunkel's partner (5)
10 Settle a score (3,4)
11 Eventually (2,3,4,3)
13 Old English coins worth five shillings (6)
14 Material for starting a fire (6)
17 The Nine Days' Queen of England in July 1553 (4,4,4)
20 Nonsense (7)
21 World's second most populous country (5)
22 Vocal composition (4)
23 Pink wading bird (8)

DOWN

1 Deep open cut (4)
2 Keepsake (7)
3 Traditional puppet show (5,3,4)
4 Cherubim, seraphim etc (6)
6 Bile-secreting organ (5)
7 Wine merchants (8)
8 Holding one's ground (8,4)
12 Cosy tale (anag) — followers (8)
15 Fine German porcelain (7)
16 Out of sorts (6)
18 Attracted (to) (5)
19 A sign of saintliness? (4)

Solution see page 241

37

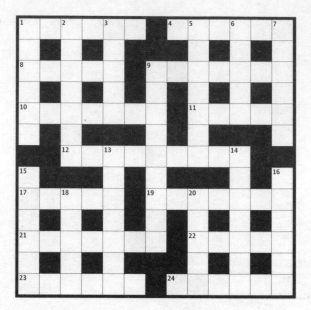

ACROSS

1 Handle clumsily (6)
4 Electricians (informal) (6)
8 Tibet's Forbidden City (5)
9 More than enough (3,4)
10 Device that measures the flow of electrical current (7)
11 Also-ran (5)
12 Sell off book stock cheaply (9)
17 Bring upon oneself (5)
19 Authentic (7)
21 Bereft (7)
22 Increase in pay (5)
23 Refuse to comply (6)
24 Carnivore — saw eel (anag) (6)

DOWN

1 Heavy short-tailed polar bird (6)
2 Country on the Bay of Bengal (7)
3 Vaulted (5)
5 Moved about restlessly and stealthily (7)
6 Trounces (5)
7 World's largest desert (6)
9 Off to bed (7,2)
13 Shows a reflection (7)
14 Dried grapes (7)
15 Lift — nick (6)
16 Edible grain (6)
18 Keeps in check (5)
20 Family of Germanic languages spoken in Scandinavia and Iceland (5)

Solution see page 242

38

ACROSS

1 Commendation (6)
4 God-fearing (5)
7 Hang around for no good reason (6)
8 Excerpt (6)
9 For his sake, words expressing annoyance! (4)
10 Recent recruit (8)
12 Avebury's prehistoric ring (5,6)
17 Sign of the zodiac (8)
19 Bound along (4)
20 Stick together (6)
21 High-altitude wispy cloud (6)
22 Vladimir Ilyich Ulyanov, d. 1924 (5)
23 Record cover (6)

DOWN

1 Skill (7)
2 Style of design popular in the 1920s and '30s (3,4)
3 National park in northern Tanzania (9)
4 Alarm (5)
5 Best in the circumstances (7)
6 African desert (6)
11 Appealingly amusing (9)
13 Make stronger (7)
14 Measure of energy in food (7)
15 Adopt (7)
16 Mischief-maker (6)
18 Broadcast for a second time (5)

Solution see page 242

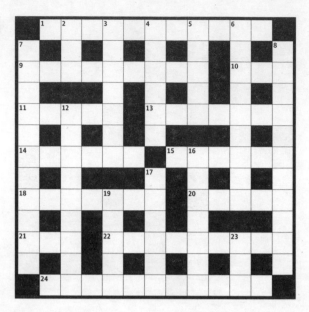

ACROSS

1 Large crate (7,4)
9 Written agreement between a country and the Vatican (9)
10 Chinese leader, d. 1976 (3)
11 Unfortunately (5)
13 Bitter conflicts (7)
14 Bind firmly together (6)
15 Sultanate in Borneo (6)
18 Remark (7)
20 Longest European river, flowing into the Caspian Sea (5)
21 Monotonous routine (3)
22 Top dog? (6,3)
24 Waste frivolously (7,4)

DOWN

2 Stiff bristle growing from an ear of barley, for example (3)
3 Indirect or cumulative effect (5-2)
4 Going without clothes (6)
5 Make provision for (5)
6 Meeting between two of the last four still in a knockout competition (4-5)
7 Stiff slip with sections covered by a film to be removed to discover if a prize has been won (7,4)
8 Lacking any interest or creativity — nepotist cad (anag) (11)
12 One's old university or school (4,5)
16 Nice region? (7)
17 Hamper (6)
19 German painter Max, a pioneer of Dada, d. 1976 (5)
23 Egg cells (3)

Solution see page 242

40

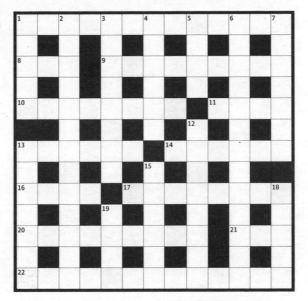

ACROSS

1 ... and no exaggeration! (2,3,2,6)
8 Conflict (3)
9 Spurge (9)
10 Street pole (that George Formby was leaning on?) (8)
11 Night shiner (4)
13 Pandemonium (6)
14 Title of Austrian and German emperors (6)
16 That's revolting! (4)
17 NCO (8)
20 Lid paint? (3,6)
21 Mummy's boy? (3)
22 Collective attack by a shiver of sharks? (7,6)

DOWN

1 It's gone wrong when this is thrown in (5)
2 Investment scam — I searched my MP (anag) (7,6)
3 Role player (8)
4 Office worker (6)
5 Stravinsky, for example? (4)
6 Nineteenth-century gaol for those who owed money (7,6)
7 Person longing (7)
12 Available staff numbers (8)
13 Dried herb from an evergreen shrub (3,4)
15 (Canine?) snack (3,3)
18 Bony and tall (5)
19 Siamese today (4)

Solution see page 242

41

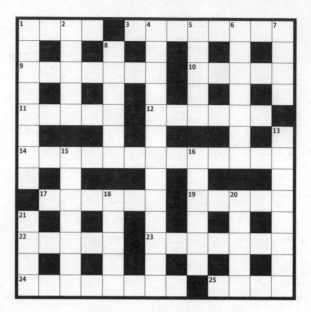

ACROSS

1 Arrived (4)
3 Puerile (8)
9 President Franklin D Roosevelt's economic policy from 1933 (3,4)
10 Longest bone in the human body (5)
11 Stagger (5)
12 Anne is (anag) — crazy (6)
14 Sweets (13)
17 One-piece full-body garment (6)
19 Scoring moves in rugby (5)
22 Diametrically opposed — very cold (5)
23 Mildly funny (7)
24 Coordinated set of clothes (8)
25 Let out (4)

DOWN

1 Fighting (8)
2 Tool for cutting grass (5)
4 Cash dispenser (informal) (4,2,3,4)
5 Elevates (5)
6 Colossal (7)
7 Damage (4)
8 Titter (3-3)
13 Faculty of vision (8)
15 Confound (7)
16 Travelling about (2,4)
18 Melee (5)
20 Vocabulary characteristic a specific group (5)
21 Duelling weapon (4)

Solution see page 243

42

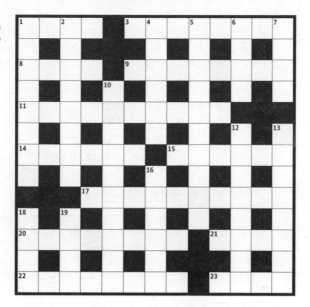

ACROSS

1 Mushy (4)
3 Pilot's control column (8)
8 That was painful! (4)
9 Marital infidelity (8)
11 Tell me the worst! (4,2,2,2)
14 Industrial action (6)
15 One and only (6)
17 Habitual (10)
20 Trencherman (8)
21 Theatrical song for solo voice (4)
22 Taking things easy (8)
23 Cone (anag) (4)

DOWN

1 Taxi Driver and Raging Bull director (8)
2 One of 12 in a pack (4,4)
4 Curio (6)
5 Lizard-like amphibian (10)
6 Wild goat with large recurved horns (4)
7 Knockout (4)
10 Combining selections from various options (4-3-3)
12 Air force unit (8)
13 Allocate a task to someone else (8)
16 Beatle John (6)
18 Food thickener (4)
19 Dartboard's centre (4)

Solution see page 243

43

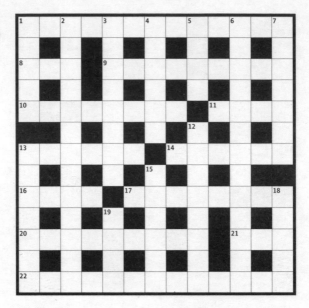

ACROSS

1 Careful thought (13)
8 Be unwell (3)
9 Release of pent-up emotions (9)
10 Defeated decisively (8)
11 Feverish chill (4)
13 Strike repeatedly with the fists (6)
14 Marred (6)
16 Come down to earth (4)
17 Metal used in strong lightweight alloys (8)
20 Swiss skeleton toboggan track (6,3)
21 Fuss (3)
22 Bitter verbal quarrel (8,5)

DOWN

1 Shoreline (5)
2 South African president, d. 2013 (6,7)
3 Enraged (8)
4 (Of two) no matter which (6)
5 ___ Smith, author of The Wealth of Nations (4)
6 Piddling (13)
7 Not a problem! (informal) (2,5)
12 Pale peat moss — human GPs (anag) (8)
13 Royal residences (7)
15 One millionth of a metre (6)
18 Loiter listlessly (5)
19 Adult male red deer (4)

Solution see page 243

44

ACROSS

1 College courtyard (10)
7 Give up (7)
8 Absolute (5)
10 Silent (4)
11 Resonant (6)
13 Debauched gatherings (6)
15 Reprobate (6)
17 Paid attention (8)
18 ___ Driver, 1976 Scorsese film (4)
21 Histrionics (5)
22 Worry intensely (7)
23 Absorbent or cushioning material (6,4)

DOWN

1 Feeling of unease (5)
2 Close adviser (4)
3 Haphazard (6)
4 Overwrought (8)
5 Deflate (3,4)
6 Cynical (4-6)
9 Reader isn't (anag) — unemotional (10)
12 Pertinent (8)
14 Nazi secret police (7)
16 Get back (6)
19 Prospero's spirit (5)
20 Dorothy's canine friend (4)

Solution see page 243

45

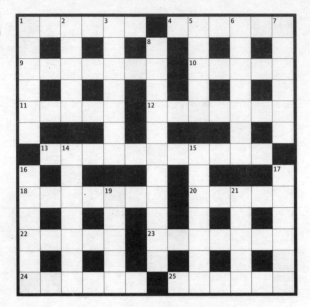

ACROSS

1 Stout (6)
4 Rain cloud (6)
9 Hopeless feeling (7)
10 Tubular pasta (5)
11 Sheer (5)
12 Knife for the end of a rifle (7)
13 No-frills (11)
18 Busy (2,3,2)
20 Means of mass communication (5)
22 Hybrid beasts of burden (5)
23 Overshadow (7)
24 Adage (6)
25 Complimentary (6)

DOWN

1 Peppery root vegetable (6)
2 Tack — abets (anag) (5)
3 Knife used in dissection (7)
5 Hint (5)
6 Windfall (7)
7 Carry out an investigation (6)
8 Bin operator (anag) — one's working on a trial basis (11)
14 Altogether (7)
15 Kind of rose (7)
16 Universe (6)
17 Documentation (6)
19 Cathedral city of North Rhine-Westphalia, seat of the Krupp industrial dynasty (5)
21 Storage facility (5)

Solution see page 244

46

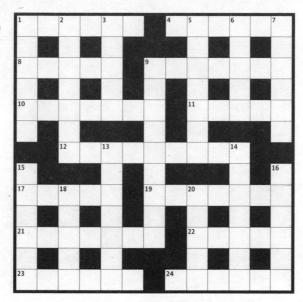

ACROSS

1 Plain — foolish (6)
4 Shun (6)
8 Volte-face (1-4)
9 Primitive eel-like fish (7)
10 Foundation (7)
11 Greek equivalent of Z (5)
12 Dummy run (9)
17 Fragment of glowing wood or coal (5)
19 Fashion accessory (7)
21 Pooter or Pepys? (7)
22 Likewise (5)
23 Somewhat (6)
24 Academic award (6)

DOWN

1 Squat (6)
2 Ramble (7)
3 Jargon (informal) (5)
5 Order to attend court (7)
6 Large number (5)
7 Ambush (6)
9 I ask hotel (anag) — without hesitating (4,1,4)
13 Admirable woman (7)
14 Crustacean (7)
15 Guard around fireplace (6)
16 Overlook (6)
18 Brag (5)
20 Remind gently (5)

Solution see page 244

47

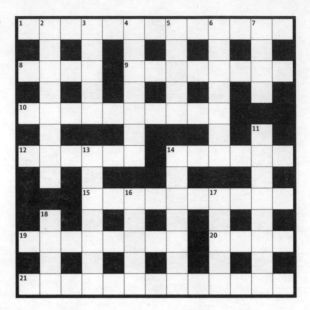

ACROSS

1 Making trivial distinctions (4-9)
8 Loose body fat (4)
9 Not absolute (8)
10 English-speaking (10)
12 Bring out — evoke (6)
14 Putty-like cement used as adhesive or filler (6)
15 Modest (10)
19 Canadian prairie province (8)
20 Necessity (4)
21 Living things (5,3,5)

DOWN

2 On the whole (3,2,3)
3 Insurgent (5)
4 Fortification consisting of a low wall (7)
5 Snow house (5)
6 Silly laughs (7)
7 Armed force (4)
11 Irish political movement (4,4)
13 Messenger (7)
14 Temporarily lost (7)
16 Agreeable odour (5)
17 Miraculous food (5)
18 Cloth spread over a coffin (4)

Solution see page 244

48

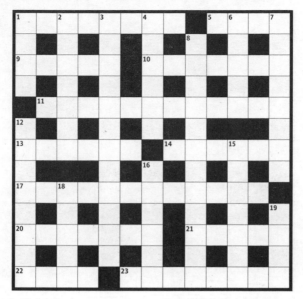

ACROSS

1 Kind of bridge (or whale) (8)
5 One's crowning glory? (4)
9 Become subject to (5)
10 Frame for creepers (7)
11 Have a drink in the local (4,3,5)
13 Knock down — tried to avoid detection (3,3)
14 Total debacle (6)
17 Energetic evangelism (informal) (5–7)
20 Fleet commander (7)
21 Poetic lament (in a country churchyard?) (5)
22 Weak and ineffectual person (4)
23 Outlook (8)

DOWN

1 Greet loudly (4)
2 Ridicule (7)
3 Totally uninterested (5,2,5)
4 Attention-grabbing (6)
6 Improvise (2,3)
7 Timber used in cabinetmaking — or so do we (anag) (8)
8 Significant rise in body temperature (12)
12 Area with lots of night spots (8)
15 Unfeigned (7)
16 Author of The Naked and the Dead, d. 2007 (6)
18 Walt Disney's young fawn (5)
19 Thin-walled cavity containing liquid (4)

Solution see page 244

49

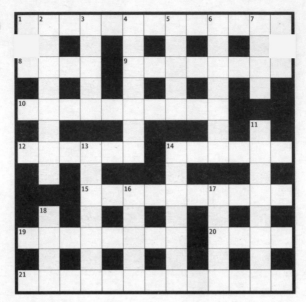

ACROSS

1 English group activity involving bells, sticks and handkerchiefs (6,7)
8 Zest — energy (4)
9 Commonness (8)
10 Secondary consequence of medical treatment (4,6)
12 Ripe (6)
14 Turmoil (6)
15 Wire-haired dog (3,7)
19 Easily frightened (8)
20 Female domestic (of all work?) (4)
21 Way to gamble on results of the weekly soccer fixtures (8,5)

DOWN

2 First (8)
3 Mischief-maker (5)
4 Tussle (7)
5 Quick (5)
6 State of disorder (7)
7 Brazils and pecans (4)
11 Military equipment and supplies (8)
13 In advance (2,5)
14 Tool (7)
16 Bantu language related to Zulu (5)
17 Shakespearean lover (5)
18 Ballpoint pen (4)

Solution see page 245

50

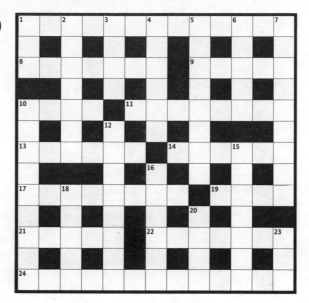

ACROSS

1 Scenic eco-trek (anag) — complex subject for boffins? (6,7)
8 Strapless top (7)
9 Kind of yellow primrose (5)
10 Passion (4)
11 Serial arrangement (8)
13 Portugal and Spain (6)
14 Two-piece swimsuit (6)
17 Pheasant, say? (4,4)
19 Surrender (4)
21 Lazybones (5)
22 Carrion feeder (7)
24 Equestrian competition involving several skills (5-3,5)

DOWN

1 Plunder (3)
2 Torrent (7)
3 Blockbuster (4)
4 Water ice (6)
5 Mohawk or Seneca, for example? (8)
6 Tights material (5)
7 Oath (9)
10 Mood of a particular time (9)
12 Off the ground (8)
15 Drink coolant (3,4)
16 Things of little importance (6)
18 Back tooth (5)
20 Aid to detection (4)
23 Juvenile newt (3)

Solution see page 245

51

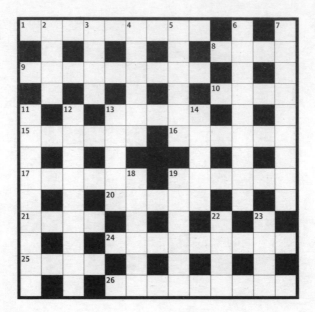

ACROSS

1 (Said) quietly (5,4)
8 White and salty goat or sheep cheese (4)
9 Big blow? (9)
10 Sell — whip (4)
13 Lobby (5)
15 Small chest for keeping valuables (6)
16 Largest city in KwaZulu-Natal (6)
17 Very warm bath (3,3)
19 German subs (1-5)
20 Daft (informal) (5)
21 Bite repeatedly (4)
24 Running nooses — link posts (anag) (9)
25 Divisible by two (4)
26 High-capacity transmission technique (9)

DOWN

2 Egg (4)
3 Ankara native? (4)
4 One coming out on top (6)
5 Preserved (6)
6 Sweet with a firm sugar coating (5,4)
7 Hard grey metal, Mn (9)
11 Sport with puck (3,6)
12 Ready to wear (3,3,3)
13 Bored and angry (3,2)
14 School — game (5)
18 Hard hat (6)
19 Thomas More's 1516 book about life on an imaginary island (6)
22 Prominent rounded hill (4)
23 Astonish (4)

Solution see page 245

52

ACROSS

5 Wish someone harm (4,3,4)
7 Apparatus used by women gymnasts (4)
8 Exceeds in height (8)
9 In one's real nature — a threat (anag) (2,5)
11 Muscular (5)
13 Breaks under tension (5)
14 Imposing residence (7)
16 Taking place every other year (8)
17 Display one's buttocks publicly (slang) (4)
18 Reply that has no relevance to what was said before (3,8)

DOWN

1 Conceal in the hand (4)
2 Intolerance (7)
3 Naval force (5)
4 Suffering (8)
5 Taking the same line of argument further (2,9)
6 Winner's ceremonial circuit of the track (3,2,6)
10 Practitioner (8)
12 Quarrel (4,3)
15 Bathroom facility (5)
17 Speechless (4)

Solution see page 245

53

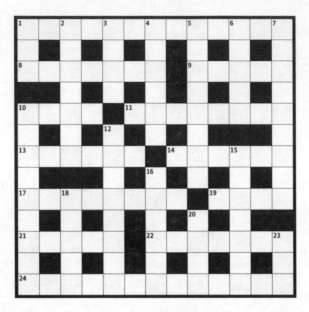

ACROSS

1 Fiftieth anniversary (6,7)
8 Cowboy's hat (7)
9 Elaine Stritch's Ladies Who ___ (5)
10 Supplied with footwear (4)
11 Old Spanish gold coin (8)
13 Andean vulture (6)
14 Major Chinese technology company (6)
17 French farewell (2,6)
19 Backhander (informal) (4)
21 On a target, the ring next to the bullseye (5)
22 Constructor (7)
24 Operetta by Franz Lehár (3,5,5)

DOWN

1 Fuel for US automobiles? (3)
2 Short rest (3-4)
3 Alleviate (4)
4 Younger (6)
5 Attack physically or verbally (8)
6 Language (informal) (5)
7 Making more attractive (9)
10 Left-winger (9)
12 Opposite (8)
15 Injured (7)
16 Feller's warning cry (6)
18 Line of mountains (5)
20 Opinion (4)
23 Uncooked (3)

Solution see page 246

54

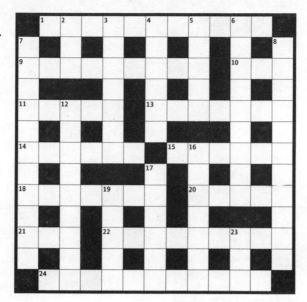

ACROSS

1 Scary (11)
9 Servant (9)
10 Contest (3)
11 Two-masted sailing vessel (5)
13 Young child (7)
14 Elaborately decorated (6)
15 Underside (6)
18 CVs (7)
20 Coordinate (3,2)
21 Gesture of agreement (3)
22 Vanilla-flavoured fizzy drink (5,4)
24 Person attracting a large audience (5-6)

DOWN

2 Decompose (3)
3 Firearm's range — no thugs (anag) (7)
4 Warm (6)
5 Observed (5)
6 Short story? (9)
7 The wrong way round (4-2-5)
8 Causing harm (11)
12 Geordie (9)
16 Plot aim (anag) — most favourable (7)
17 Napping (6)
19 Large and showy Latin American parrot (5)
23 Be indebted (to) (3)

Solution see page 246

55

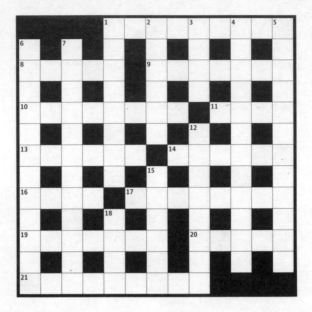

ACROSS

1 Come down with a bump? (5-4)
8 Tipped (5)
9 Performs again (7)
10 Punished (6,2)
11 Fuss (2-2)
13 German composer, d. 1883 (6)
14 Small basket for measuring fruit (6)
16 Reveal — command (4)
17 High-ranking bureaucrat (8)
19 The race (anag) — unit of area (7)
20 Plant with daisy-like flowers (5)
21 Cavaliers (9)

DOWN

1 Road safety devices (8)
2 Quick and skilful (6)
3 English-born US comedian, d. 2003 (4)
4 Extremely tense person (1,3,2,6)
5 Restless and unhappy (12)
6 Employee who wants to leave dead on time (5-7)
7 Cheerfully irresponsible (5-2-5)
12 Alfresco (8)
15 Light-hearted fun (6)
18 Impertinence (4)

Solution see page 246

56

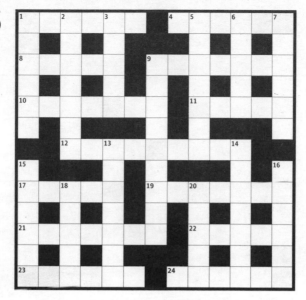

ACROSS

1 Push or bump roughly against someone (6)
4 Close-fitting necklace (6)
8 Blow one's own trumpet (5)
9 From Valencia or Malaga? (7)
10 Blow up (7)
11 Thoughts (5)
12 Excellent — best possible (3–6)
17 Put entirely inside something else (5)
19 Raw pickled herring fillet (7)
21 Space to stretch out when sitting (7)
22 Ward off (5)
23 Makes little adjustments (6)
24 Communicative (6)

DOWN

1 Prattle (6)
2 Small onion-like bulb used for seasoning (7)
3 Not now! (5)
5 Curative (7)
6 Stab (5)
7 Present again with just the odd change (6)
9 Metal instrument (5,4)
13 Field for horses (7)
14 Great storm (7)
15 Shot — slug (6)
16 Suffering from acne (6)
18 Brass instrument (5)
20 Lead (5)

Solution see page 246

ACROSS

1 Using frugally (10)
7 Dispute over territory between rival gangs (4,3)
8 Spore-producing organisms (5)
10 Dry outer covering of some seeds (4)
11 Highest spot in Britain (3,5)
13 Stay (6)
15 Poetically, a gentle wind (6)
17 Indian city, centre of the Sikh faith (8)
18 Unencumbered (4)
21 Long (5)
22 Perfectly delightful (7)
23 Mickey Mouse creator (4,6)

DOWN

1 Egyptian god of the sky (5)
2 Stitched (4)
3 Better ventilated (6)
4 Protector (8)
5 Ancient city on the Tigris (7)
6 Prepared for action (2,3,5)
9 Rebellion (10)
12 Well-defined (8)
14 Inland Turkish sea between the Dardanelles and the Bosporus (7)
16 Largest island of French Polynesia (6)
19 Receive and pass on (5)
20 Greenish-blue colour (4)

Solution see page 247

58

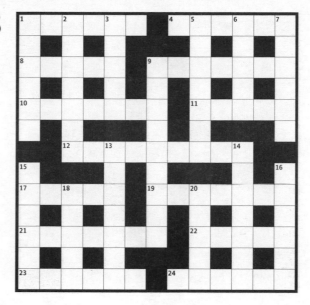

ACROSS

1 National park in south-west England (6)
4 Handwriting (6)
8 Personal strong suit (5)
9 Valour (7)
10 Greedy eater (7)
11 Divulge (3,2)
12 Meet (9)
17 Back-office work (abbr) (5)
19 Deep rumbling sound (7)
21 Croesus (anag) — sweetening agent (7)
22 Business transactions (5)
23 Lots and lots (6)
24 SI unit of force (6)

DOWN

1 Sculpted figure of a person (6)
2 Canvas pavilion (7)
3 Open (5)
5 Garland for the head (7)
6 Clumsy (5)
7 Doing one's best? (6)
9 Upholstered bench (9)
13 Instrument panel (7)
14 Glowing (7)
15 Horse-drawn cab (6)
16 Jail (6)
18 Nasal secretion (5)
20 Excessive (5)

Solution see page 247

59

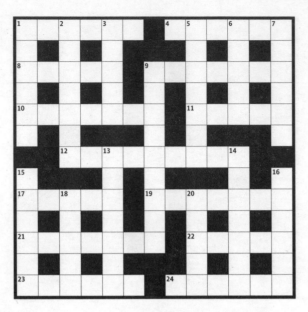

ACROSS

1 Concerning each of two or more people (6)

4 Heart-rending (6)

8 Principles that cannot be contested (5)

9 In a punctual manner (7)

10 Underwater swimmer in a rubber suit (7)

11 Clumsy (5)

12 Division of the Bible (9)

17 Seventeen-syllable poem (5)

19 Person moved away from a dangerous place (7)

21 Prevent from being discovered (7)

22 Production company's dogsbody (5)

23 Computer allowing access to the network (6)

24 Bee or ant? (6)

DOWN

1 Fielding position near the bowler (3-3)

2 Small vessel used for moving ships (7)

3 Warning device (5)

5 Come to understand (7)

6 Filth — music genre (5)

7 Small North American wolf (6)

9 Seem slightly familiar (4,1,4)

13 Squash (7)

14 Fungus scratched for by pigs (7)

15 Removes from the shell — I'm disappointed! (6)

16 Search through very thoroughly (6)

18 Intimate (5)

20 Gas, Ar (5)

Solution see page 247

60

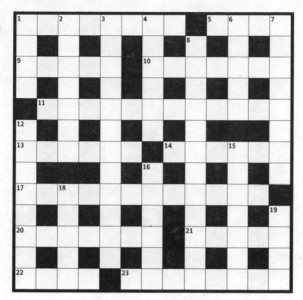

ACROSS

1 To my way of thinking (2,2,4)
5 Written musical symbol indicating pitch (4)
9 Melted together (5)
10 Shutdown (7)
11 Proficient (12)
13 Spoke (6)
14 Shipping forecast area (6)
17 Quite frequently (2,5,2,3)
20 Predicament (7)
21 Senseless (5)
22 Nearly hopeless (4)
23 Broken piece (8)

DOWN

1 Gen (abbr) (4)
2 Tuneful (7)
3 Await a favourable moment (4,4,4)
4 Inhabit (6)
6 Chuckle (5)
7 Diabolical (8)
8 Be lively and enjoyable (2,4,1,5)
12 Left high and dry (8)
15 Place for a ship to make fast (7)
16 Inequitable (6)
18 Fuel tanker (5)
19 Special skill (4)

Solution see page 247

61

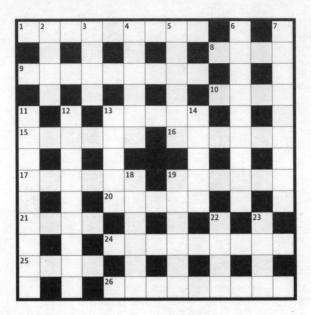

ACROSS

1 Friction (9)
8 American wild cat (4)
9 Broken French (informal) (9)
10 Butter used in Indian cookery (4)
13 Invalidate (5)
15 Fruit — shade (6)
16 Skewer (6)
17 Manipulate balls (6)
19 Reconnoitre (6)
20 Run off to get married (5)
21 Sage (4)
24 Bowdlerise (9)
25 Branch part (4)
26 Preserve by lowering temperature (6–3)

DOWN

2 Dull studious type (4)
3 Coquette (4)
4 Type of hospital drip (6)
5 Cause to make a mistake (4,2)
6 Skill(s) attained while living in uncultivated country (9)
7 Audacious (9)
11 Name all forms of a verb (9)
12 Composure (9)
13 Supple (5)
14 Supple (5)
18 It could supposedly change base metals into gold (6)
19 Fir (6)
22 Nasty giant (4)
23 Asterisk (4)

Solution see page 248

62

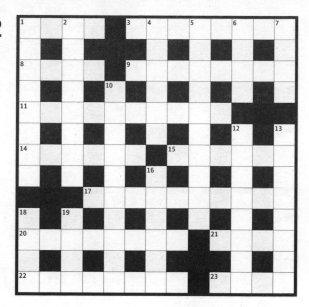

ACROSS

1 Be furious (4)
3 White wine and soda water (8)
8 Fiver, say (4)
9 From the very beginning (3,5)
11 WInd gauge (10)
14 Oesophagus (6)
15 Projectile (6)
17 Not fitting (10)
20 Group of atoms bonded together (8)
21 Hair style (abbr) (4)
22 Pertinent (8)
23 Nicholas II was the last (4)

DOWN

1 Lively Spanish dance (8)
2 Maternal (8)
4 Young hen (6)
5 Short of what is required (10)
6 Video communications system (4)
7 Be furious (4)
10 Polish astronomer d. 1543 (10)
12 Blessing (anag) — slickness of speech (8)
13 Long flag — bad cold (8)
16 Fish (red or grey) (6)
18 Lady Hamilton or Lady Thompson? (4)
19 Cut with shears (4)

Solution see page 248

63

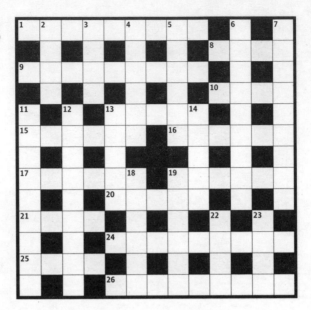

ACROSS

1 Astronomer's instrument (9)
8 Right to another's property, if an obligation is not discharged (4)
9 Captivated (9)
10 Pygmalion playwright (4)
13 Swift (5)
15 Pointer (6)
16 Protective covering (6)
17 Confused sound of many voices (6)
19 Self-centred person (6)
20 Approximate (5)
21 Stratagem (4)
24 Alternatively (9)
25 Cheerio (2-2)
26 Squinting (5-4)

DOWN

2 Paradise (4)
3 Vile (anag) — really bad (4)
4 Unpleasant laugh (6)
5 Bits (6)
6 Baltic country (9)
7 Perfectly pure — fairytale heroine (4,5)
11 Hermit (9)
12 Wordiness (9)
13 Miller's product (5)
14 Upper leg (5)
18 Straw hat (6)
19 Exit (6)
22 Affectedly quaint (4)
23 Expression of dawning comprehension (1,3)

Solution see page 248

64

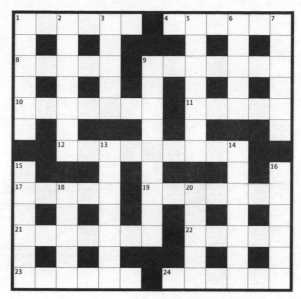

ACROSS

1 Next to (6)
4 Piece of jewellery (6)
8 Saying (5)
9 School bag (7)
10 Up in the air (2,5)
11 Minister to (5)
12 Office — factory (9)
17 Catalogues (5)
19 Quick — exact (7)
21 Cinchona bark extract used to treat malaria (7)
22 Make amends (5)
23 Value (6)
24 Stand-in ruler (6)

DOWN

1 Nut (from South America?) (6)
2 Ingest (7)
3 Fantasy (5)
5 Do a turn (anag) — circular domed building (7)
6 Distinct (5)
7 Occupant (6)
9 Outstanding example (9)
13 Short break (7)
14 Monstrosity (7)
15 Inner circle (6)
16 Upward slope (6)
18 Go round the edge (5)
20 Helping of food (5)

Solution see page 248

65

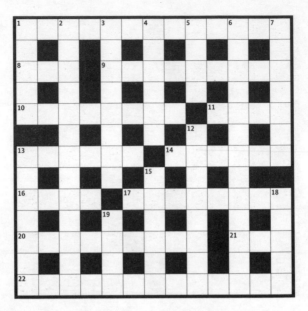

ACROSS

1 All dolled up — liked oldsters (anag) (7,2,4)
8 Identity disc (3)
9 Become engaged? (9)
10 Bald (8)
11 Substantial branch from a tree trunk (4)
13 Egyptian riddler? (6)
14 Frisson (6)
16 Highest point (4)
17 Persuade by flattery (4-4)
20 Protestant followers of a German theologian, d. 1546 (9)
21 Unpleasantly cold and damp (3)
22 Machine for writing text (4,9)

DOWN

1 Drop (5)
2 Dog — serenest light (anag) (7,6)
3 Aircraft that can land on snow (3-5)
4 Loathe (6)
5 For us (4)
6 Items used for pressing (7,6)
7 Sympathetic (7)
12 Mild aversion (8)
13 Superficial (7)
15 Murphy (informal) (6)
18 Physical strength (5)
19 Large brown seaweed (4)

Solution see page 249

66

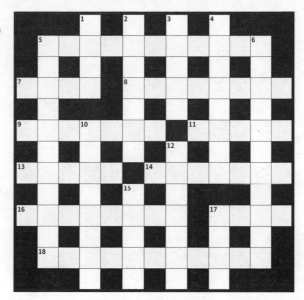

ACROSS

5 Healing (11)
7 Commotion (4)
8 Immortal (8)
9 Similes (anag) — weapon (7)
11 Save up for future use (5)
13 Feeble (5)
14 Daydream (7)
16 Encouragement (8)
17 Gloat (4)
18 Shakiness (11)

DOWN

1 Swerve (4)
2 Touchy-feely (7)
3 French woman (sometimes fatale) (5)
4 Reliable (8)
5 1955 Little Richard hit (5,6)
6 Information detailing patient's illness (4,7)
10 Scuffle (8)
12 Legal action (7)
15 Suggest — drift (5)
17 Loop (4)

Solution see page 249

67

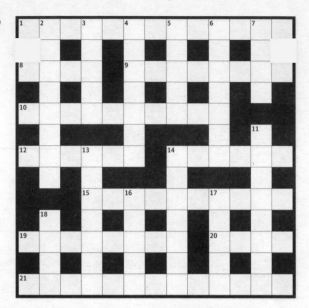

ACROSS

1 Nasdaq, for example (5,8)
8 Short written message (4)
9 Lightest gas (8)
10 Large kingfisher (aka laughing jackass) (10)
12 Repeat mindlessly (6)
14 Prime of life (6)
15 Safari, for example (3,7)
19 Bulldoze (8)
20 Mark an 'X' (4)
21 Pallet picker-upper (8,5)

DOWN

2 Not touching a drop (8)
3 Criminal (5)
4 Display (7)
5 Apple drink (5)
6 Deviation from the norm (7)
7 Great pleasure (4)
11 August (8)
13 Fitting that serves as fulcrum for an oar (7)
14 Construction worker's helmet (4,3)
16 Russian pancake served with caviar and sour cream (5)
17 Hesitate (5)
18 Leander's lover, who committed suicide when he drowned (4)

Solution see page 249

68

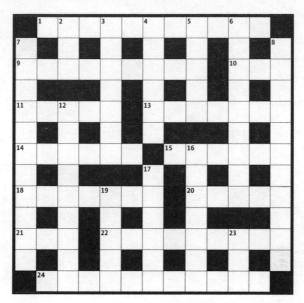

ACROSS

1 Nifty device (11)
9 Commotion (3,3,3)
10 Organised (3)
11 Folded back part of coat collar (5)
13 Enormous (7)
14 Length of step (6)
15 Halfway (6)
18 Puzzle (7)
20 Rigged (5)
21 Stop (3)
22 A good one stops to help (9)
24 Shocking — tea in salons (anag) (11)

DOWN

2 Be in arrears (3)
3 Messy (7)
4 Financial gain (6)
5 Deep chasm (5)
6 Filing system (4,5)
7 Bertrand Russell, for instance (11)
8 Self-governing (11)
12 Tip grader (anag) — bird (9)
16 Conflagration (7)
17 Not liable (6)
19 Continues (5)
23 It could be high or cream (3)

Solution see page 249

69

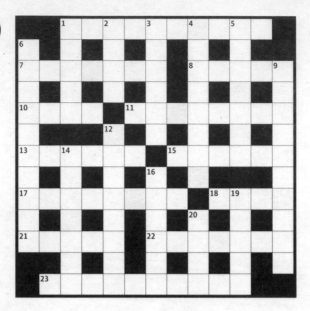

ACROSS

1 Feign death (4,6)
7 Sunshade (7)
8 Sanctioned (5)
10 Town crier's call (4)
11 Political philosophy based on avoiding extremes (8)
13 Eyrie resident (6)
15 Immediately! (6)
17 Unmoving (8)
18 Equitable (4)
21 Damp (5)
22 Seasonal wind (south-west or north-east) of southern Asia (7)
23 Swimming underwater without breathing equipment (4,6)

DOWN

1 Cleanse (5)
2 Besides (4)
3 Nick (6)
4 Good for you (8)
5 Smarm — balm (7)
6 A slip of the tongue? — no promises (anag) (10)
9 Shaken instrument (10)
12 Not sanctioned (8)
14 PR stunt? (7)
16 Former students (6)
19 In the middle of (5)
20 Against (4)

Solution see page 250

ACROSS

1 Unwell (4)
3 Unable to think clearly (8)
9 Puffed up and vain (7)
10 Hair (5)
11 Foul in snooker (2-3)
12 Kind of bomb (6)
14 Spring bulb with blue flowers — cheating harpy (anag) (5,8)
17 One using hook, line and sinker? (6)
19 Indian statesman, d. 1964, father of Mrs Indira Gandhi (5)
22 Take (an exam) again (5)
23 Without weapons (7)
24 Precious stones (8)
25 Russian emperor (4)

DOWN

1 Young trees (8)
2 Small group of musicians (5)
4 In a weak position (2,5,6)
5 Book size (5)
6 Part (7)
7 Sprint (4)
8 Thick cushion for sitting on (6)
13 Meat joint (8)
15 Memory loss (7)
16 Heavy sailcloth (6)
18 Housey-housey (5)
20 Organic matter in soil (5)
21 Jab — nudge (4)

Solution see page 250

71

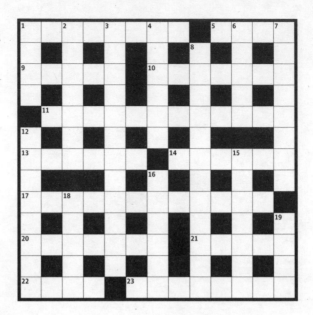

ACROSS

1 Spherical fungus (8)
5 Pace (4)
9 Round of gunfire (5)
10 Affliction (7)
11 Sentry's challenge (3,4,5)
13 Something strange (6)
14 Characteristic of the countryside (6)
17 Type of Christian — best in prayer (anag) (12)
20 Shoulder blade (7)
21 Whinny (5)
22 Herb used in pickles (4)
23 Emphasised (8)

DOWN

1 Route through mountains (4)
2 Pilfered (7)
3 Caused (7,5)
4 Brood of young born to an animal (6)
6 Data arranged in rows and columns (5)
7 Make-believe (8)
8 Capital of Haiti (4-2-6)
12 Calm (8)
15 Sycophants (7)
16 Finally (2,4)
18 Internet message(s) (5)
19 Discard (4)

Solution see page 250

72

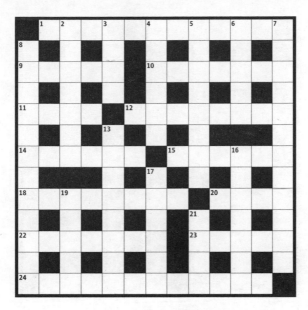

ACROSS

1 One who talks too much (12)
9 Ring-shaped coral reef (5)
10 City of the central Netherlands (7)
11 Eyelid attachment (4)
12 Enrol to vote (8)
14 King of the Fairies (6)
15 Closed political meeting (6)
18 Many (8)
20 Knife (4)
22 Close associate (7)
23 From which a mighty tree could grow! (5)
24 Resistant to liquid (12)

DOWN

2 Dekko (4-3)
3 Daring (4)
4 Avoided (6)
5 Sweet almond paste (8)
6 Full length (5)
7 Traditional Good Friday fare (3,5,4)
8 Writing instrument (9,3)
13 Handle (8)
16 French car (7)
17 Book page size (6)
19 Eejit (5)
21 Side post of a doorway (4)

Solution see page 250

73

ACROSS

1 West German chancellor, 1969-74 (6)

4 Small pop group (5)

7 Small mouthful (6)

8 Playfully makes fun of (6)

9 Male parent of a horse, for example (4)

10 Clothing business (informal) (3,5)

12 Profuse bleeding (11)

17 Special significance (8)

19 Giant who eats people (4)

20 In truth (6)

21 Beat by cunning (6)

22 Devotion to religious principles (5)

23 Cash in shares, bonds etc (6)

DOWN

1 Given to reading (7)

2 Grim — a US tree (anag) (7)

3 In a state of wild excitement (9)

4 Large box used for storage (5)

5 Hardy wild horse of the American western plains (7)

6 Forced out of office (6)

11 Rotating wheel used in navigation systems (9)

13 Placate by making concessions (7)

14 Evangelist (7)

15 Irritatingly catchy tune (7)

16 Endure cheerfully (4,2)

18 Mixture of two or more metals (5)

Solution see page 251

74

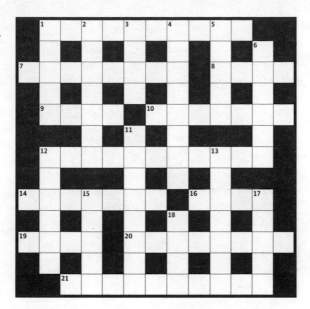

ACROSS

1 Crawlers (10)
7 High-handed (8)
8 Traditional naval drink (until 1970) (4)
9 Satisfy completely (4)
10 Sad young hopeful trying to emulate a role model (informal) (7)
12 High-pitched sound expressing lust (4,7)
14 Belly (7)
16 Interrogate (4)
19 Down (4)
20 6 January celebration of the Three Wise Men's visit to the baby Jesus (8)
21 Kind of printer — eyelid wash (anag) (5,5)

DOWN

1 Seabirds of the cormorant family (5)
2 Of the shoreline (7)
3 Brace (4)
4 Sea facing Venice (8)
5 Big cat hybrid (5)
6 Sound made by a turkey cock (6)
11 Hair plucker (8)
12 Lack of stability (6)
13 Difficult problem (7)
15 Drama with singers and orchestra (5)
17 Of an area (5)
18 Outlook (4)

Solution see page 251

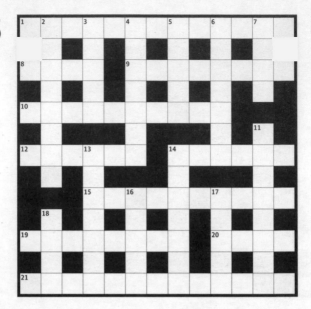

ACROSS

1 Selfish (13)
8 Reddish-brown colour (4)
9 Give up (8)
10 Not ideal (6,4)
12 Solid (6)
14 One who holds forth (6)
15 Solo (10)
19 Merchant (8)
20 Winding spool on a fishing rod (4)
21 Group that does each other favours — not rowdy bloke (anag) (3,3,7)

DOWN

2 Disgust (8)
3 Go one better than (5)
4 Support (5,2)
5 Dimwit (5)
6 Boat racing event (7)
7 Farewell (informal) (2-2)
11 Ancestor (8)
13 Leafstalks usually cooked, sweetened and eaten in puddings (7)
14 Abide by — watch (7)
16 Soothe (5)
17 The Turn of the ___ , 1898 Henry James horror story (5)
18 Legendary Swiss crossbowman and folk hero (4)

76

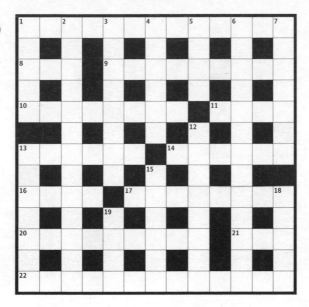

ACROSS

1 Causing disappointment after an impressive start (13)
8 Natural material from which metals can be extracted (3)
9 Disrespectful behaviour (9)
10 Rum and lime juice cocktail (8)
11 Sudden rush of wind (4)
13 Insubstantial (6)
14 Dried grape (6)
16 Clothes (informal) (4)
17 Offer as a sacrifice by burning (8)
20 Egg-laying (9)
21 Intestines (3)
22 Prevents things getting out of hand (5,3,3,2)

DOWN

1 Shy away from (5)
2 Position that's very exposed to attack (3,6,4)
3 Like a close-knit and unfriendly group (8)
4 Put in (6)
5 A friendly and reliable country (4)
6 People gossiped (7,6)
7 Be unfaithful to one's partner (5,2)
12 Conveyer belt for arriving air travellers' luggage (8)
13 Joint just above a horse's hoof — to fleck (anag) (7)
15 Dance slowly while in an embrace (6)
18 Have a meal at home (3,2)
19 South-east Asian country (4)

Solution see page 251

77

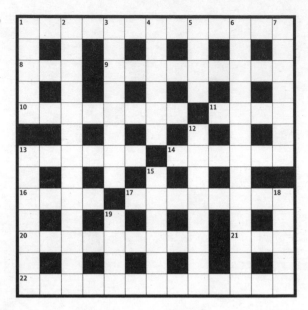

ACROSS

1 Attention-seeking behaviour (13)
8 Silence — joke (3)
9 Relating to government (9)
10 Adolescent (8)
11 Skip (4)
13 Smartly turned out (6)
14 In Ancient Greece, gazing into her eyes was petrifying! (6)
16 State of feeling (4)
17 Relish (8)
20 Occurring at three-yearly intervals (9)
21 Behave unnaturally (3)
22 Entrenched (4-2-3-4)

DOWN

1 Roget (anag) — plant disease (5)
2 Dynamite (4,9)
3 Aircraft such as the de Havilland Tiger Moth (8)
4 ___ Girls, chorus line dancers (6)
5 Cereal (4)
6 Unable to have contact with other people (13)
7 Citizen army (7)
12 Military wake-up call (8)
13 Downgraded (7)
15 Orthopaedic immobilising device (6)
18 Praise (5)
19 Hostile to (4)

Solution see page 252

78

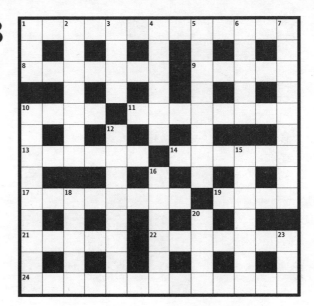

ACROSS

1 Clean up — noted at cinema (anag) (13)
8 Remote settlement (7)
9 Soup spoon (5)
10 Separate — component (4)
11 At a bargain price (3,1,4)
13 Soup dish (6)
14 Pathetic (6)
17 Imaginary (8)
19 Swivel (4)
21 Similar (5)
22 Live in (7)
24 Went about seeking votes (13)

DOWN

1 Couple (3)
2 Professional provider of food etc (7)
3 Sheltered spot (4)
4 Battle (6)
5 Unfortunate (3–5)
6 Sound recording (5)
7 Always fresh (9)
10 Autocratic ruler (9)
12 Suggestive (8)
15 Cry (informal) (7)
16 Kind of cotton cloth (6)
18 String (5)
20 Part of a drum brake (4)
23 Smidgen (3)

Solution see page 252

79

ACROSS

1 Beauty treatment (6)
4 Transparently clear (5)
7 Known and esteemed (6)
8 Field event (6)
9 Multitude — MC (4)
10 Friendly and sociable (8)
12 One who popularises a fashion (11)
17 Delicate ornamental metalwork (8)
19 Venomous snakes (4)
20 Detestation (6)
21 Publish — annoy (3,3)
22 Enid Blyton character (5)
23 Not level (6)

DOWN

1 At top speed (4,3)
2 Gleeful chuckle (7)
3 Runaway (9)
4 Saying what is 23 (5)
5 Addictive drug (7)
6 Aim — decorative pattern (6)
11 Immediately after that (9)
13 Akin (7)
14 Kitchen appliance (7)
15 State of bliss (7)
16 Tall breed of hound with a long silky coat (6)
18 Nerdish (5)

Solution see page 252

80

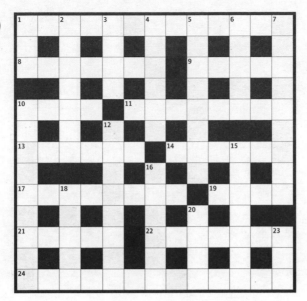

ACROSS

1 Pre-decimal British coin (10,3)
8 Done away with (7)
9 Scottish child (5)
10 Goatee location (4)
11 Abundantly productive (8)
13 Take for granted (6)
14 Plaster used to coat walls (6)
17 Loose dressing gown (8)
19 I don't know the answer (4)
21 Put up with (5)
22 Cure for all ills (7)
24 Thievish (5-8)

DOWN

1 Liquid used for preserving timber (3)
2 Ashes (7)
3 Desire to have something that is possessed by another (4)
4 Last — bear (6)
5 Aristocracy (8)
6 Instructions given for a task (5)
7 Dogged — unyielding (9)
10 Flexible body armour (5,4)
12 At hand (8)
15 Opportunist (7)
16 City of ancient Greece with an oracle (6)
18 Peer Gynt Suite composer (5)
20 Unforeseen obstacle (4)
23 Assistance (3)

Solution see page 252

81

ACROSS

1 Pontificate (6)
4 Evade (5)
7 Mellifluous (6)
8 Group within a group (6)
9 School payment(s), for example (4)
10 Vague talk and empty promises (8)
12 Subversive element working for the opposition (6,5)
17 Curry dish — Avon lido (anag) (8)
19 Weep copiously (4)
20 Deodorant applicator (4-2)
21 Heavily populated island in the Gulf of Naples (6)
22 Communal fund (5)
23 Dangerous (6)

DOWN

1 Wise (7)
2 Prominent cubist (7)
3 Feline cry (9)
4 Uncertainty (5)
5 Areas like the Sahara (7)
6 Lure (6)
11 Like Emperor Haile Selassie? (9)
13 Curl of hair (7)
14 1938 novel, starting: 'Last night I dreamt I went to Manderley again' (7)
15 Well read (7)
16 Czech composer, d. 1904 (6)
18 Kind of aunt? (5)

Solution see page 253

82

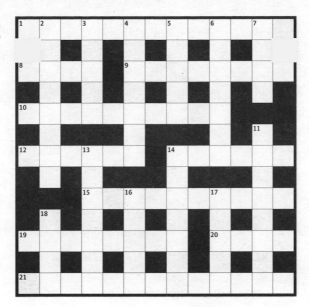

ACROSS

1 Christian organisation with brass bands (9,4)

8 Poet exiled from Rome in AD 8 by Emperor Augustus (4)

9 Memorial (8)

10 Apocalyptic battle (10)

12 Treacherous people (with ladders?) (6)

14 Trig ratio (6)

15 Composer of Oliver! (6,4)

19 Mythical reptile with a lethal look (8)

20 Miniature whirlpool (4)

21 Dishonest behaviour (7-6)

DOWN

2 French region of many dormant volcanoes, capital Clermont-Ferrand (8)

3 Clear spirit from Poland, Russia and Sweden, made mainly of water and ethanol (5)

4 Beams (that may be shivered?) (7)

5 Admitted (to wrongdoing) (5)

6 Nuts used to make marzipan (7)

7 Producer of coins (4)

11 Uninvited visitor (8)

13 Extremely funny (slang) (7)

14 Medical examination (5-2)

16 Rosie (anag) — willow (5)

17 Short holiday (5)

18 Three Wise Men (4)

Solution see page 253

83

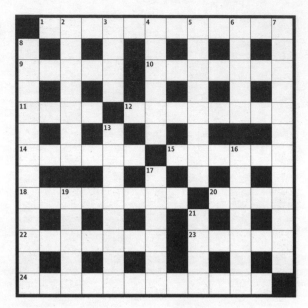

ACROSS

1 Specious financial saving (5,7)
9 Intoxicating (5)
10 Excellent (7)
11 Ninth letter of the Greek alphabet (4)
12 Italian bubbly (8)
14 Listlessness (6)
15 Dreadful pong (6)
18 Intellectual (8)
20 Percussion instrument (4)
22 Withdrawal (7)
23 Atmospheric gas shielding us from ultraviolet radiation (5)
24 With steady and rapid gain (4,4,4)

DOWN

2 Kind of electric plug (7)
3 River of Hades (4)
4 Accompany (6)
5 Antithesis (8)
6 Spirit measure (5)
7 Species of European bunting (12)
8 New Zealand's second largest city (12)
13 Broad-brimmed Mexican hat (8)
16 Jittery (7)
17 Container for liquid (6)
19 Make progress (3,2)

Solution see page 253

84

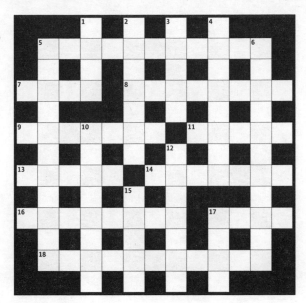

ACROSS

5 Booby prize (6,5)

7 Of a dull greenish-brown colour (4)

8 Acquiring knowledge (8)

9 Absent from work because of illness (3,4)

11 Courted (5)

13 Old coin worth four pence (5)

14 From Valletta, perhaps (7)

16 Bamboozle (8)

17 Male — something that stops here? (4)

18 Unpleasant (11)

DOWN

1 Search thoroughly (4)

2 Marital state (7)

3 Customary (5)

4 Discovered (5,3)

5 Verbatim (4,3,4)

6 Ridiculous (11)

10 Slipshod (8)

12 Trading places (7)

15 Backless couch (5)

17 Enthusiast (4)

Solution see page 253

85

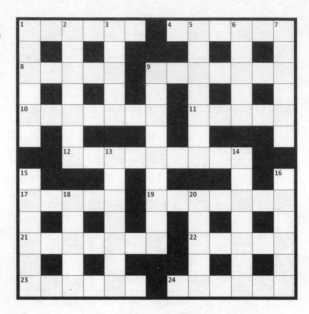

ACROSS

1 Shack (6)
4 Location finder (6)
8 Odious (5)
9 Wood polish (7)
10 Without a success (7)
11 Trunk (5)
12 Short lively piece of music with improvisation (9)
17 Detach (5)
19 Jack, American writer, a pioneer of the beat generation, d. 1969 (7)
21 Disregard (7)
22 Great (American) (5)
23 Oxygenise (6)
24 Slogan (6)

DOWN

1 Muscular (6)
2 Poison — ices ran (anag) (7)
3 Herb related to mint (5)
5 Sterile (7)
6 Fresher (5)
7 Broadcast opinions? (3,3)
9 Licence to board public road transport (3,6)
13 Caustic — strong smelling (7)
14 Ostentatiously rich (7)
15 21 shillings (pre-decimal) (6)
16 Sea monster devouring sailors trying to escape from Charybdis (6)
18 Device that bleeps to draw one's attention (5)
20 Member of a cult based on a belief that Haile Selassie was the Messiah (5)

Solution see page 254

86

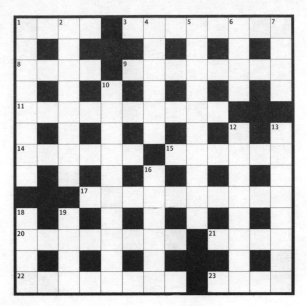

ACROSS

1 Actuality (4)
3 About to happen (8)
8 Plough (4)
9 High-ranking army officer (5,3)
11 One's wife (informal) (3,7)
14 Blockhead (6)
15 Object used in fighting (6)
17 Done by people acting together (10)
20 First performance (8)
21 Pound — lump of chewing tobacco (4)
22 Place of residence (8)
23 Suggestive (4)

DOWN

1 Attractive (8)
2 Speed (8)
4 Leave stranded with little hope of rescue (6)
5 Rebellion (10)
6 Genuine — honest (4)
7 Young children — shorts (4)
10 Avoiding the company of others (10)
12 Natural ability (8)
13 Meant (for each other?) (8)
16 Old two-bob bit (6)
18 Moved quickly (4)
19 Pool — pure and simple (4)

Solution see page 254

ACROSS

1 Pudding made with milk and gelatin (10)
7 Special assignment (7)
8 Loose rocks on a mountainside (5)
10 Fasten — hair (4)
11 Direct hit (5,3)
13 Chest for valuables (6)
15 Go away! (4,2)
17 Wave (8)
18 Asian and Australian starling with a loud call (4)
21 Cast out (5)
22 Moral (7)
23 To be kept safe (10)

DOWN

1 Crude (5)
2 Waterless (4)
3 Agree (6)
4 Vindicated (8)
5 Something to be worn (7)
6 Relentless (10)
9 At last (10)
12 Cap or beanie, for instance (8)
14 Staying power (7)
16 Wealth (6)
19 Boat used for cruising or racing (5)
20 Cold-shoulder (4)

88

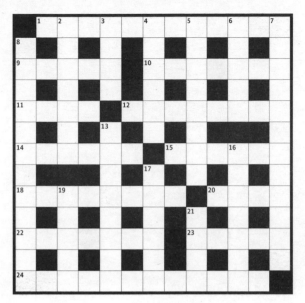

ACROSS

1 Pampered pooch (Parisian?) (6,6)
9 Gamut (5)
10 Wild ox in the US (7)
11 Digital covering (4)
12 Excess of revenue over expenses (4,4)
14 1.5 litre wine bottle (6)
15 São Salvador, Bahia became its first capital in 1549 (6)
18 Observing (8)
20 Stony waste matter (in a heap?) (4)
22 Dismissal (informal) (5-2)
23 Optical device (5)
24 Old crime of stealing objects of little value (5,7)

DOWN

2 Hierarchical position (7)
3 Requirement (4)
4 Covering for the middle of a wheel (6)
5 Located abroad (to avoid domestic tax) (8)
6 Speak in lazy manner (5)
7 Match at Boris's old school, played on St Andrew's Day (4,4,4)
8 Negotiating tactic of taking things to the limit (12)
13 Medical charlatanism (8)
16 Very large number (7)
17 Long-haired Turkish cat or rabbit (6)
19 Extended area of land (5)
21 Magnificent (4)

Solution see page 254

89

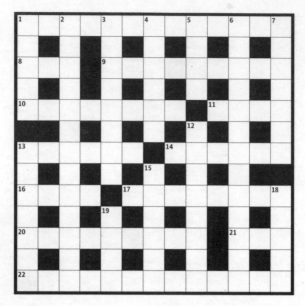

ACROSS

1 Where ants help (anag) —
   long-nosed insectivore (8,5)
8 Nervous twitch (3)
9 Convert (9)
10 Mental disorder (8)
11 Lump of earth (4)
13 In the existing circumstances
   (2,2,2)
14 Water gate (6)
16 Tear (4)
17 Feeling blissful happiness (8)
20 Making an appearance (7,2)
21 Vein structure in a leaf (3)
22 European principality (13)

DOWN

1 Devoured (5)
2 Area where entry is not
   permitted (9,4)
3 Mesmerising (8)
4 Sexual intercourse (slang) (6)
5 River at Aviemore (4)
6 British armed service (5,3,5)
7 Cajole (7)
12 Egg-laying mammal (8)
13 Spray can (7)
15 Hound dog (6)
18 Room on board (5)
19 Burbot or turbot? (4)

Solution see page 255

90

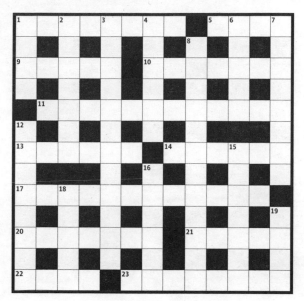

ACROSS

1 Detested (8)
5 Peaceful (4)
9 Language of southern India and Sri Lanka (5)
10 Heavy iron lever (7)
11 My Way singer (5,7)
13 Metallic element used in alloys, Os (6)
14 Distinguishing mark — prestige (6)
17 Type of sofa (6,6)
20 Belgian port (7)
21 Greek epic poem about the siege of Troy (5)
22 Hearing aids? (4)
23 Start shooting (4,4)

DOWN

1 Vocal range (4)
2 Far from exciting (7)
3 Given up (12)
4 Surfeit (6)
6 Head of a community of monks (5)
7 Holmes's arch-enemy (8)
8 Puma (8,4)
12 Secret meeting (8)
15 Hungarian-born escapologist, d. 1926 (7)
16 Make a mistake (4,2)
18 Modify (5)
19 Boundary (4)

Solution see page 255

91

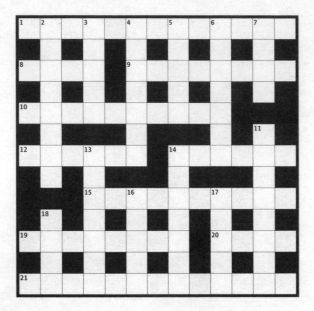

ACROSS

1 Queenly attendants — small tarts (5,2,6)
8 Functions (4)
9 Without a sound (8)
10 Lake District lake, the largest in England (10)
12 Monster perhaps living in a Scottish lake (informal) (6)
14 Bavaria in German (6)
15 Irish elf (10)
19 Sliced cured beef (8)
20 Principal (4)
21 Action taken without prior knowledge of the consequences (4,2,3,4)

DOWN

2 Attacked (8)
3 Given medicine (5)
4 Watch attentively (7)
5 Cut into two equal pieces (5)
6 Convent (7)
7 Far from fair (4)
11 Casino employee (8)
13 Separate (5,2)
14 Flaw (7)
16 Unadorned (5)
17 Muggy (5)
18 Labyrinth (4)

Solution see page 255

92

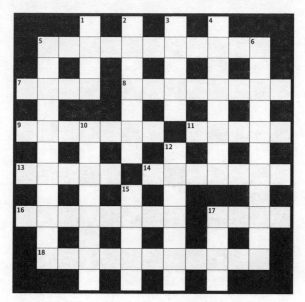

ACROSS

5 Travelling from place to place (11)
7 Smallest particle of an element (4)
8 Ailments (anag) (4,4)
9 Wriggle — wrangle (7)
11 Suit (5)
13 Full formal evening dress for men (5)
14 Complain bitterly (against) (7)
16 From the beginning (Latin) (2,6)
17 Very dry and pale sherry (4)
18 One-act Gilbert and Sullivan opera (5,2,4)

DOWN

1 Neat — prune (4)
2 Early Christian missionary (7)
3 Motionless (5)
4 Wild rush of frightened animals (8)
5 Beatrix Potter character (5,6)
6 Eventuality (11)
10 Magnificent (8)
12 Word opposite in meaning (7)
15 No longer fresh (5)
17 Constant change (4)

Solution see page 255

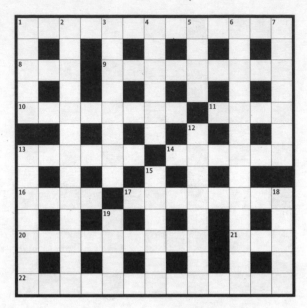

ACROSS

1 Responsibility for observing developments (8,5)
8 Edge (3)
9 Gripe (9)
10 Taking an oath (8)
11 Kiss and cuddle (informal) (4)
13 Not moving (6)
14 Commotion (6)
16 Impressed deeply (4)
17 Spanish vegetable soup, served cold (8)
20 Procession of cars (9)
21 ___ Gershwin, lyricist (3)
22 British patriotic song (4,9)

DOWN

1 Merchandise (5)
2 Given to mood changes (13)
3 Poetic name for Ireland (8)
4 Stockings (6)
5 Inlets (4)
6 Together (2,11)
7 Goods in transport (7)
12 Writ compelling attendance in court (8)
13 Prison (slang) (7)
15 South-east African country, formerly Nyasaland (6)
18 Michelle or Barack? (5)
19 Child's bed (4)

Solution see page 256

94

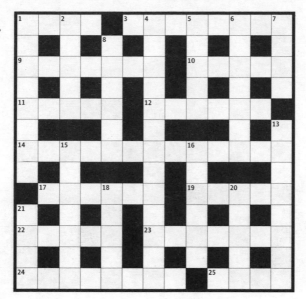

ACROSS

1 Worst — as good as can be (4)
3 Probably (1,4,3)
9 Food fish (3,4)
10 Small medicine bottle (5)
11 Faithful (5)
12 Be a sign of (6)
14 Force the person responsible to explain what happened (4,2,7)
17 Stress on a syllable (6)
19 Gangway (5)
22 Possessed (5)
23 Risk-taker (7)
24 Exciting adventure (8)
25 Glorify (4)

DOWN

1 Large place of worship (8)
2 Frightening (5)
4 Socially deprived (13)
5 Come to maturity (5)
6 Chinese dog similar to a Pekingese (4-3)
7 Christmas (4)
8 Thoroughly unreliable person (3,3)
13 Alfred the Great's brother and predecessor, d. 871 — the elder (anag) (8)
15 Conical (anag) — brief and to the point (7)
16 Unpleasantly damp and sticky (6)
18 Find oneself eventually (3,2)
20 Spicy Mexican sauce (5)
21 Warning cry by a golfer (4)

Solution see page 256

95

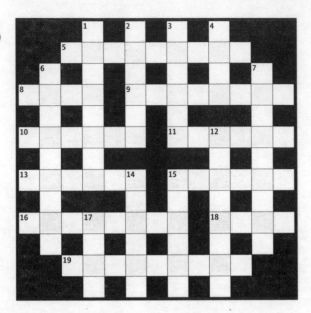

ACROSS

5 Target of abuse (4,5)

8 Period of calm (4)

9 One who looks on the bright side (8)

10 German dramatist, Bertold, d. 1956 (6)

11 City in Lombardy (where Romeo goes when banished from Verona) (6)

13 Draw back with sudden pain (6)

15 Shooting star (6)

16 Mild-mannered and easy-going person (8)

18 The History ___ (Alan Bennett play) (4)

19 Unable to pay creditors (9)

DOWN

1 Innkeeper (8)

2 Without profit to the seller (2,4)

3 Small fowl (6)

4 Dejected (4)

6 Peevish (9)

7 Assumed name (9)

12 NB (4,4)

14 Greatest fighter in the defence of Troy against the Greeks (6)

15 Purpose — incentive (6)

17 Seashore grit (4)

Solution see page 256

96

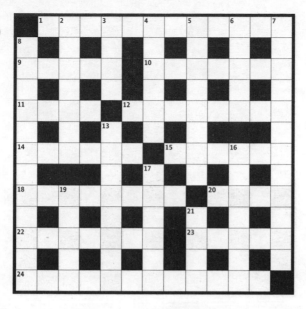

ACROSS

1 Lowered area between stage and audience (9,3)
9 Way beyond the norm (5)
10 Affinity (7)
11 Dingy (4)
12 Melancholy (8)
14 Involve (6)
15 Autocrat (6)
18 Someone who interprets or explains (8)
20 Get anxious (4)
22 Digging deep (7)
23 Learner (5)
24 Spies working for more than one side (6,6)

DOWN

2 Withdraw (7)
3 Prank (4)
4 Homily (6)
5 News hound (8)
6 Verification (5)
7 Gossip (6-6)
8 Confused (6-6)
13 Every second year (8)
16 Low wall around a balcony (7)
17 Riddle (6)
19 Rice dish cooked with meat, fish or vegetables etc (5)
21 East end of a church, containing the altar (4)

Solution see page 256

97

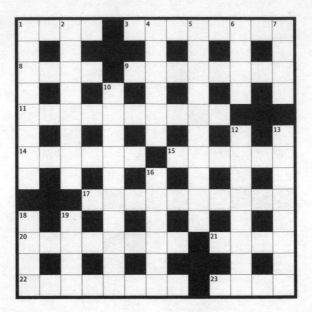

ACROSS

1 Adorn (4)
3 Author of The Da Vinci Code (3,5)
8 Cut of meat (4)
9 Disinterested (8)
11 Singular (10)
14 Extremely small (6)
15 Come over the horizon (6)
17 Catastrophic (10)
20 Investigate (4,4)
21 Walk through shallow water (4)
22 Much loved and valued person (8)
23 Cried (4)

DOWN

1 Belt of calms and light winds in the Atlantic and Pacific (8)
2 Burrowing ground squirrel (8)
4 Plant that completes its life cycle within 12 months (6)
5 Riders' route (10)
6 Expel (4)
7 Point of intersection (4)
10 Tips (10)
12 Soft drink (8)
13 Shape of the waxing moon (8)
16 Fried fish coating (6)
18 Level (4)
19 Strong thick cord (4)

Solution see page 257

98

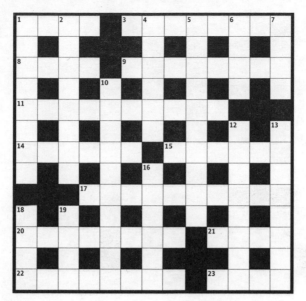

ACROSS

1 Disguise (4)
3 Young person over twelve (8)
8 Speak indistinctly (4)
9 Albumen (3,5)
11 Hollywood (10)
14 With it (6)
15 Passion (6)
17 Be responsible for a false start (4,3,3)
20 Sudanese capital (8)
21 English church architect, d. 1723 (4)
22 Blood vessels (8)
23 Lose velocity (4)

DOWN

1 Declare wrongly (8)
2 Misspend (8)
4 The Henry who fathered Elizabeth I (6)
5 Warranting a wider audience (10)
6 Way of walking (4)
7 Great Barrier formation? (4)
10 One searching for suitable candidates for a job (10)
12 William McGonagall's kind of poetry? (8)
13 In mint condition (5,3)
16 Tidy — tree (6)
18 Lady's finger (4)
19 Diplomacy (4)

Solution see page 257

99

ACROSS

1 Very full (6)
4 Musician (5)
7 Souk (6)
8 The ___ and the Carpenter (Lewis Carroll poem) (6)
9 Secret language (4)
10 Marine exhibition (8)
12 Get seriously to work (7,4)
17 Waste (8)
19 British peer (4)
20 Artificial (6)
21 Interval (6)
22 Money (slang) (5)
23 Past (6)

DOWN

1 Showy person (7)
2 Large French country house (7)
3 Set aside (9)
4 Italian luxury fashion house, established 1913 (5)
5 Scope (7)
6 Short summary (6)
11 Not of this world (9)
13 Non-partisan (7)
14 Aromatic herb (7)
15 Tend to (7)
16 Handy (6)
18 Emotionally demanding? (5)

Solution see page 257

100

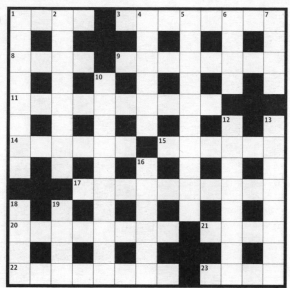

ACROSS

1 Mention and identify (4)
3 Lower jawbone (8)
8 Well ventilated (4)
9 Game with pitchers (8)
11 Balkan country on the Adriatic (10)
14 Small edible crustacean (6)
15 Depressing experience (6)
17 Solid figure with eight plane faces (10)
20 Discourteous (8)
21 Brandy–like spirit distilled from grape residue (4)
22 Behind (in France) (8)
23 Uncouth youth (informal) (4)

DOWN

1 Accident narrowly avoided (4,4)
2 Sailors (8)
4 Gobsmacked (6)
5 Firmly established (4-6)
6 Prejudice (4)
7 Fish (often jellied) (4)
10 Pasta in long slender threads (10)
12 Earnest plea (8)
13 Hence rag (anag) — red wine grape (8)
16 (Proverbially mad) milliner (6)
18 Intellect (4)
19 Incentive (4)

Solution see page 257

101

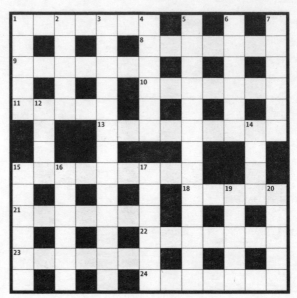

ACROSS

1 Saviour (7)
8 On the way (2,5)
9 Alter (7)
10 Lauded (7)
11 Hits with an open hand (5)
13 Twirl like a ballerina (9)
15 Historical record (9)
18 Exhausted (5)
21 Make comprehensible (7)
22 Idea (7)
23 Spanish gentleman (7)
24 Provoked (7)

DOWN

1 Fundamental values of a group (5)
2 Dance, originally from Brazil (5)
3 Absolutely necessary (13)
4 Assistant (6)
5 Collection of delightful things (8,5)
6 Beginning (6)
7 Old poorhouse official (eg Mr Bumble) (6)
12 Luxuriant (4)
14 Record (4)
15 Day nursery (6)
16 Fast-flowing part of a river (6)
17 Swiss state (6)
19 Fit for a king (5)
20 Old-fashioned (5)

Solution see page 258

102

ACROSS

1 HEADGEAR? (4)
3 Trounced (8)
9 Agricultural tool shaped like a pickaxe (7)
10 Small hammer (under which things may be sold) (5)
11 Swiss mathematician, d. 1783 (5)
12 Accessible by computer (6)
14 Sweets collectively (13)
17 1960 Hitchcock film (6)
19 Mode of transport (5)
22 Spotted scavenger (5)
23 Tortilla — I or Burt (anag) (7)
24 Weary (8)
25 Garden of England (4)

DOWN

1 Start (8)
2 Flower part (5)
4 Act in a way likely to cause a problem (3,3,7)
5 Business magnate (5)
6 Malicious retaliation (7)
7 Uninteresting (4)
8 Unrefined (6)
13 Becoming extinct (5,3)
15 Beginning to develop (7)
16 Clamour (6)
18 Noise of metal on metal (5)
20 Still breathing (5)
21 Raymond Blanc, for example (4)

Solution see page 258

103

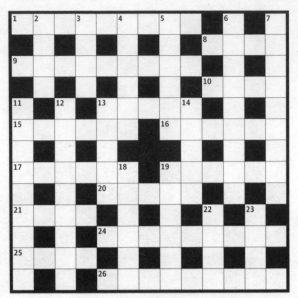

ACROSS

1 Highly detailed (9)
8 Repast (4)
9 Keep down costs (9)
10 Where the altar is found in a church (4)
13 Precipitous (5)
15 Dissimilar (6)
16 Legal (6)
17 Board ship (6)
19 Small restaurant (6)
20 Reasonable judgement (5)
21 Rowing team (4)
24 Trembled (9)
25 Christmas (4)
26 Full stiff petticoat worn under a skirt (9)

DOWN

2 Shortage (4)
3 Explosion (4)
4 Stand-offish (6)
5 Ornamental tuft of threads (6)
6 Take a silly risk (5,4)
7 Aristocratic descent (4,5)
11 Inactive — quit scene (anag) (9)
12 Walloped (9)
13 Sound of the bagpipes (5)
14 Lose one's cool (5)
18 Genuine and legitimate (informal) (6)
19 Commanded (6)
22 Prison accommodation (4)
23 Shaped as with an axe (4)

Solution see page 258

104

ACROSS

5 Unkempt (11)
7 Hair style (4)
8 Plot — love affair (8)
9 Hired (7)
11 Attack — girl (5)
13 Smooth (5)
14 Rhythm (7)
16 Headquarters of the US Defense Department (8)
17 Protective cover (4)
18 Stone coffin (11)

DOWN

1 Former legal restraining order (4)
2 Genteel (7)
3 Minor (5)
4 Final (8)
5 Unarmed (11)
6 Two-time (6–5)
10 Hole (8)
12 Pot-bellied (7)
15 Incite (3,2)
17 Euphoric (4)

Solution see page 258

105

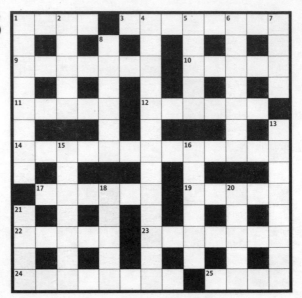

ACROSS

1 Insects (4)
3 Duplicitous (3–5)
9 Come down (7)
10 When expected (2,3)
11 Frown angrily (5)
12 Meaty soup (6)
14 Giving up criminal activities (5,8)
17 Geronimo's people (6)
19 Code for R (5)
22 Love affair (5)
23 Finder of a magic lamp (7)
24 Memento (8)
25 Potter's material (4)

DOWN

1 Intentionally (2,6)
2 Vigorous and enthusiastic enjoyment (5)
4 Off target (4,2,3,4)
5 Rime (5)
6 Riding a bike (7)
7 Squirrel's nest (4)
8 Artificial limb (informal) (3,3)
13 Lawyer (8)
15 Get better (7)
16 Overseas (6)
18 Army unit (5)
20 Mannequin (5)
21 Rear — endorse (4)

Solution see page 259

106

ACROSS

1 Discourage (3,3)
4 Monk's garb (5)
7 Rather — with less delay (6)
8 Runner-up's award (6)
9 Enthusiastic enjoyment (4)
10 Mad, bad Roman emperor, assassinated AD 41 (8)
12 Study and collection of coins (11)
17 Team game with sticks (8)
19 Fall in drops (4)
20 £10 (6)
21 Do something as a favour (6)
22 Austrian symphony composer, d. 1809 (5)
23 Header (anag) (6)

DOWN

1 Essential dietary requirement (7)
2 A Christmas Carol character (4,3)
3 Predictions (9)
4 Country forming the western part of Hispaniola, independent since 1804 (5)
5 Temporary encampment (7)
6 Jungle hero created by Edgar Rice Burroughs (6)
11 Type of tenure (9)
13 Eerie (7)
14 Gratify one's appetites (7)
15 Mass of small rounded pebbles (7)
16 Brood of chicks (6)
18 Large expanse of water (5)

Solution see page 259

107

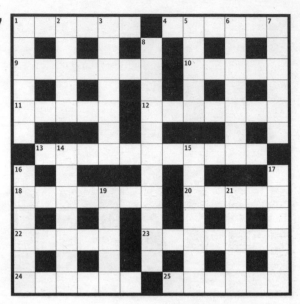

ACROSS

1 Easter ___ , 1948 film with Judy Garland and Fred Astaire (6)
4 Led (6)
9 Level out (7)
10 Roofing slabs (5)
11 Flexible (5)
12 Coach (7)
13 Strikingly different (11)
18 Long-suffering (7)
20 Solo (5)
22 Between (5)
23 Places of business (7)
24 Company (6)
25 Condition caused by lack of vitamin C (6)

DOWN

1 Learners (6)
2 Retaliate (5)
3 Most profound (7)
5 Spare (5)
6 Small-toothed whale, larger than a porpoise (7)
7 Win over (6)
8 Calculation — or tacit snub (anag) (11)
14 End result (7)
15 Deal illegally (7)
16 Jumped suddenly (6)
17 Largest of the Channel Islands (6)
19 Rowing crew (5)
21 Crop up (5)

Solution see page 259

108

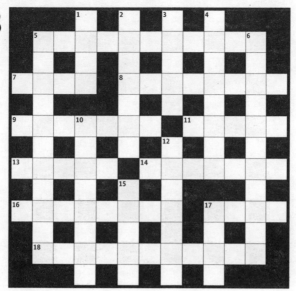

ACROSS

5 Polite form of words to attract attention (2,3,6)

7 Short drive in a car (4)

8 Part of a cruciform church — patterns (anag) (8)

9 Russian revolutionary, assassinated, 1940 (7)

11 Special set of circumstances (5)

13 Defect (5)

14 Non-standard dialect from Newcastle-upon-Tyne (7)

16 Member of the radio audience (8)

17 Nub (4)

18 Crowd body movements at a sporting event (7,4)

DOWN

1 City at the confluence of the Saône and Rhône (4)

2 Filmed scene not appearing in the final cut (3-4)

3 Plaintive cry (5)

4 Festival celebrating the exodus of the Israelites from Egypt (8)

5 Policy of a country seeking to extend its control over others (11)

6 Outlay (11)

10 1970s' news and information service, like Ceefax and Prestel (8)

12 Trial (7)

15 Special way of doing something (5)

17 Landlocked central African country, capital N'Djamena (4)

Solution see page 259

109

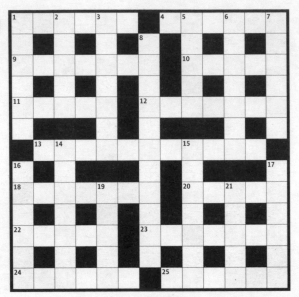

ACROSS

1 French port opposite Kent (6)
4 Drug, such as morphine (6)
9 Japanese art form — I'm a giro (rev) (7)
10 Secret store (5)
11 Release (3,2)
12 Cooking utensil (7)
13 A super stick (anag) — North American tree cultivated for its lightweight timber (5,6)
18 Small pasta cases with savoury fillings (7)
20 Arbour (5)
22 Unsophisticated (5)
23 Irritable (7)
24 Line on a cricket pitch (6)
25 WH Auden's first name (6)

DOWN

1 Absent-minded drawing (6)
2 Be (5)
3 Ornamental fowl (7)
5 Ski slope (5)
6 Lacking in colour or vitality (7)
7 Urge strongly and sincerely (6)
8 US river and state (11)
14 Bill (7)
15 Heist (7)
16 Humorously mocking (6)
17 Ragamuffin (6)
19 Portents (5)
21 18th-century card game, the forerunner of bridge (5)

Solution see page 260

110

ACROSS

1 Recklessly extravagant (10)
7 Boxing (8)
8 Containing a lot of fat, eggs and sugar (4)
9 Tub (4)
10 Hard yellow Swiss cheese (7)
12 Easily angered (3-8)
14 Acrobat — glass (7)
16 Swindle (4)
19 Hospital unit (4)
20 Completely free of dirt (8)
21 Everyday language (10)

DOWN

1 Fathom (5)
2 Left out (7)
3 Produced an egg (4)
4 Gelatinous sweeties (8)
5 Linger (5)
6 Frightened (6)
11 Barrie character (5,3)
12 Himalayan kingdom (6)
13 Concert performance (7)
15 Move (5)
17 Child (5)
18 Metal alloyed with copper to make brass (4)

Solution see page 260

111

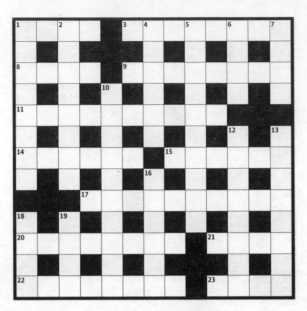

ACROSS

1 Jolly joke (4)
3 The adventures of Captain Kirk? (4,4)
8 Care for (4)
9 Wooden house (3,5)
11 Straying from the party line (3-7)
14 One of Jupiter's moons (6)
15 Area that's the commercial heart of Venice (6)
17 Theatre stage (10)
20 Yobbo (8)
21 French bread (4)
22 You needn't thank me (3,2,3)
23 Sell (4)

DOWN

1 Festive party (8)
2 Sleeveless dress, like an apron (8)
4 Chinese philosophical system based on the teachings of Lao-tzu (6)
5 Generally accepted (10)
6 Red gem (4)
7 Sharp twist (4)
10 Aromatic leaves, used for flavouring (10)
12 Last — mutilate (anag) (8)
13 Was at one (with) (8)
16 Attack (6)
18 Bottom of one's face (4)
19 Chimney dirt (4)

Solution see page 260

112

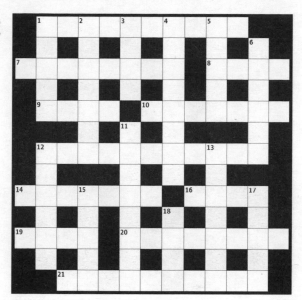

ACROSS

1 Campanologist (4,6)
7 Prophesy (8)
8 Cleans — bottle (4)
9 Sunk fence (2–2)
10 Container for coal (7)
12 Modish (11)
14 Bluebottle (7)
16 Drinking places (frequented by barristers?) (4)
19 Viral infection (4)
20 Tip (8)
21 Showing curiosity (10)

DOWN

1 Market stall — Lincoln's assassin (5)
2 Bloodsuckers (7)
3 Wander (4)
4 Becoming aware of (8)
5 Fungal disease of cereals (5)
6 Labour prime minister, d. 1967 (6)
11 Conversation (8)
12 Don (6)
13 Feast (7)
15 Make broader (5)
17 Indulged to the full (5)
18 Food fish (4)

Solution see page 260

113

ACROSS

1 Zimbabwean president, 1987-2017 (6)
4 Boy's name — a long way (5)
7 Fights (6)
8 Pollen-producing part of a flower (6)
9 Yemen's chief port (4)
10 Okayed (8)
12 Not properly tuned (11)
17 Postponed (8)
19 Highly strung (4)
20 Slackness (6)
21 Pay back (6)
22 Unfortunately (5)
23 Poisonous snakes (6)

DOWN

1 Road surface (7)
2 Light anchor — real GNP (anag) (7)
3 Non-participant (9)
4 Of small importance (5)
5 Normandy port (2,5)
6 Walk with long steps (6)
11 Looted (9)
13 Attached (7)
14 Foot-operated lever (7)
15 Stray from the subject (7)
16 Grown-ups (6)
18 Irritable (5)

Solution see page 261

114

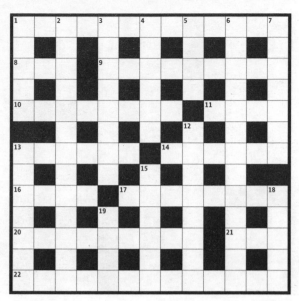

ACROSS

1 Tropical fish — heckler at a jet (anag) (13)

8 Humour (3)

9 Oneself? (6,3)

10 Extortionate payment demanded from a tenant (4,4)

11 Where Bonnie Prince Charlie fled after his defeat at Culloden (4)

13 Skimpy (6)

14 Brass band instrument (6)

16 Awkward and stupid person (4)

17 Liquid fuel (8)

20 Luxury cabin on a liner (9)

21 Optic organ (3)

22 Culloden (1746), for example (7,6)

DOWN

1 Take down (5)

2 Drug hindering blood clotting (13)

3 (Of an office holder) unpaid (8)

4 Gypsy language (6)

5 Just some (1,3)

6 Indirect result (5-2,6)

7 After that (7)

12 Blood poisoning from a local bacterial infection (8)

13 Cissy (informal) — limps OK (anag) (7)

15 King of England, January–October, 1066 (6)

18 Sister's daughter (5)

19 Cain and Abel's younger brother (4)

Solution see page 261

115

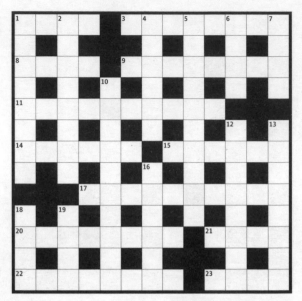

ACROSS

1 Den (4)
3 Versatile employee (8)
8 Cop shop (4)
9 Repeated without understanding (8)
11 Lawless adventurer (10)
14 They can never win (6)
15 Military engagement (6)
17 Propitious (10)
20 Spring–flowering bulb (8)
21 In the same place (Latin; abbr) (4)
22 Casual footwear (8)
23 Prolonged mutual hostility (4)

DOWN

1 Low area where waste is buried (8)
2 Augment (8)
4 South American river (6)
5 Sixty (10)
6 One of four art galleries in England (4)
7 Constructed (4)
10 Anomaly — a Breton air (anag) (10)
12 South-east African country (8)
13 Not properly cared for (8)
16 Nurse — nursery rhyme doctor (6)
18 Knackered (4)
19 US agency responsible for space flight (4)

Solution see page 261

116

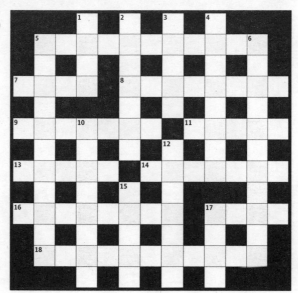

ACROSS

5 Treasured assets (5,6)
7 Suspicious (4)
8 Often (8)
9 Sender of unwanted emails (7)
11 Teutonic god in the Ring Cycle (5)
13 Provocation (informal) (5)
14 Female performer (7)
16 Fabric — cry 'odour' (anag) (8)
17 Avenging deity (4)
18 Petty (5–6)

DOWN

1 Cramped (informal) (4)
2 Passed legislation (7)
3 Squalid (5)
4 Start time (4,4)
5 Flying targets? (4,/)
6 Poised and confident — US lass freed (anag) (4–7)
10 A girdle round the earth? (8)
12 Kind of paint (7)
15 Very good — fish (5)
17 Disappear gradually (4)

Solution see page 261

117

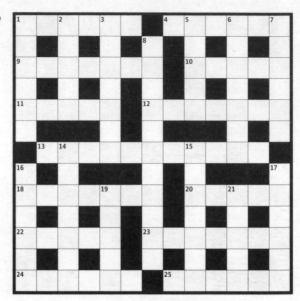

ACROSS

1 Preserve in brine or vinegar (6)

4 They're served to add moisture or taste to food (6)

9 Italian electrical engineer, d. 1937 (7)

10 Central areas in buildings; open to the sky (5)

11 Fourth letter of Greek alphabet (5)

12 Insulated container for food and drink from the fridge (4,3)

13 Chaos (11)

18 Robbery at gunpoint (5-2)

20 Social blunder (5)

22 Indian side dish of yogurt and chopped cucumber (5)

23 Models' pathway (7)

24 Chaos (6)

25 Put down (6)

DOWN

1 Hair dressing (6)

2 Song celebrating the birth of Jesus (5)

3 Garment worn by ballet dancers (7)

5 1836 massacre at a San Antonio, Texas mission (5)

6 Large North American deer (7)

7 Kind of story about a dog? (6)

8 Cautious (11)

14 Sourness (7)

15 Dress for bed (7)

16 Retreat — a marsh (anag) (6)

17 Sap (6)

19 Jack (5)

21 Supporting structure (5)

Solution see page 262

118

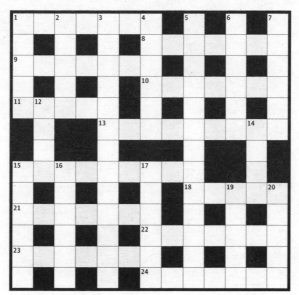

ACROSS

1 Shrub with berries used to flavour gin (7)

8 In a shrewd way (7)

9 Unit of explosive power (7)

10 Tooth doctor (7)

11 Rapid simultaneous shooting (5)

13 Luxurious car (with a chauffeur?) (9)

15 Go to sleep! (6,3)

18 Violent disturbance (5)

21 Behaved dishonestly (7)

22 Nero or I (anag) — from which a common metal comes (4,3)

23 It's offensively ugly (7)

24 Hovering singer (7)

DOWN

1 The first king of England and Scotland (5)

2 First name of the British prime minister since 2019 (5)

3 Place to fill the tank (6,7)

4 Unsystematic (6)

5 Hum yon quartet (anag) — basic explanation of all modern physics (7,6)

6 Sign of the zodiac (6)

7 Evergreen shrub with white flowers (6)

12 German-based supermarket chain (4)

14 Hopeless (informal) (2,2)

15 Growth found on tree trunks and rocks (6)

16 Bloke (6)

17 Once popular songs (often golden) (6)

19 Bowed instrument slightly larger than a violin (5)

20 Examine (5)

Solution see page 262

119

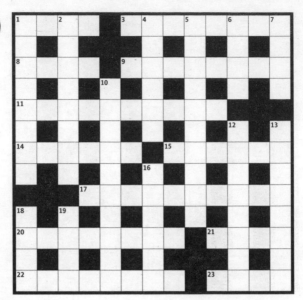

ACROSS

1 Gather — food (4)
3 Paid regularly (8)
8 Hebridean island, where in 563 St Columba founded a monastery (4)
9 Nemo's vessel (8)
11 Aid to getting dressed (10)
14 They can usually manage — old horse-dealers (6)
15 Statement (6)
17 Volume booster — he'll air duo (anag) (4,6)
20 Banana-like fruit (8)
21 Founding queen of Carthage (did next to nothing!) (4)
22 Cheapest accommodations on old passenger ships (8)
23 Gets older (4)

DOWN

1 Traffic jam (8)
2 War memorial (8)
4 Lack of interest in things in general (6)
5 Design style used by Charles Rennie Mackintosh, say (3,7)
6 Out of work (4)
7 Sprinkle — powder (4)
10 Imposing item of bedroom furniture (4-6)
12 Bulge (8)
13 Splendid (8)
16 Border (6)
18 Mimics — primates (4)
19 Jar for cut flowers (4)

Solution see page 262

120

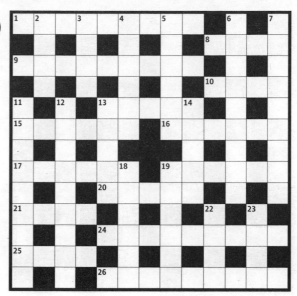

ACROSS

1 Clever idea (9)
8 And others (2,2)
9 Shoe polisher (9)
10 Look at inappropriately (4)
13 School student (5)
15 Percussion instrument (6)
16 Fungus that produces mould on damp material (6)
17 Rapidly rotating star, emitting electromagnetic waves very quickly (6)
19 Insect that feeds on plant products (6)
20 Lower one cannot get! (5)
21 Rock music with gloomy lyrics (4)
24 Basic preparations (9)
25 With great skill (4)
26 When viewing figures are highest (5,4)

DOWN

2 Defraud — crow (4)
3 Keen on (4)
4 Deliberately disobedient (6)
5 Dupe (6)
6 Jump by a performer on to the concert audience below (5-4)
7 Move unconsciously? (9)
11 Whipping boy (9)
12 Polite conversation on trivial matters (5,4)
13 One who does not acknowledge your god(s) (5)
14 Dark reddish brown (5)
18 Performer chanting rhyming lyrics to African–American music (6)
19 Sensible thinking (6)
22 Hit a wasp or fly (4)
23 Dreadful (4)

Solution see page 262

121

ACROSS

1 Possibility (6)
4 Police trainee (5)
7 Pleasure craft —
old ape (anag) (6)
8 Fast cat — fast car (6)
9 Consequently (4)
10 Engage an electrical device (6,2)
12 Number that's of interest to hay
fever sufferers (6,5)
17 Frankly — that's outrageous! (8)
19 Item resting on stumps (4)
20 Dependable (6)
21 Rubber (6)
22 Sweet — money (5)
23 Way (6)

DOWN

1 Don't be so glum! (5,2)
2 Having a run of luck (2,1,4)
3 Ship lookout's position (5,4)
4 Ship — art (5)
5 French king's eldest son (7)
6 Authoritarian (6)
11 Urge to travel (5,4)
13 Costly footballing error (3,4)
14 Annoyance (7)
15 Britannia's weapon (7)
16 Tool with a flat cutting edge (6)
18 Gleaming (5)

Solution see page 263

122

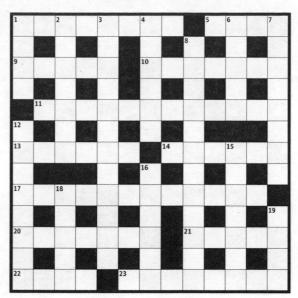

ACROSS

1 Facial hair (8)
5 Develop (4)
9 Stolen (5)
10 Hinged window blind (7)
11 24 June (9,3)
13 Valuable little piece (6)
14 Ten a penny (6)
17 Arousing violent feelings (12)
20 Warm and friendly (7)
21 Parent's brother (5)
22 Objectives (4)
23 Obstinate (8)

DOWN

1 Unit of electric power (4)
2 Glimmer of understanding (7)
3 Lucky Jim author (8,4)
4 Start again after a break (6)
6 Assessed (5)
7 Causing anxiety (8)
8 Practical guidelines (5,2,5)
12 Surround (8)
15 African country — leather (7)
16 Charm worn to ward off evil (6)
18 Sacked (5)
19 Spotted (4)

Solution see page 263

123

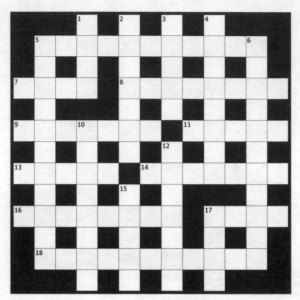

ACROSS

5 A turf event (4,7)

7 Scottish family (4)

8 Island just south of Corsica (8)

9 Baffle (7)

11 Giddy — silly (5)

13 Monastery (5)

14 As 'happy' is to 'sad' or 'long' is to 'short' (7)

16 Thread used in surgery to stop internal bleeding (8)

17 Four-wheel-drive general purpose vehicle (4)

18 Item banged when seeking entry (4,7)

DOWN

1 Read over quickly (4)

2 Beauty (7)

3 Lively — slightly drunk (5)

4 One coming from Manila? (8)

5 Revolving window screen (6,5)

6 Dangerous animal, native to North America (7,4)

10 Peering–through–fingers game (8)

12 Cover completely (7)

15 Tremor (5)

17 Gag (4)

Solution see page 263

124

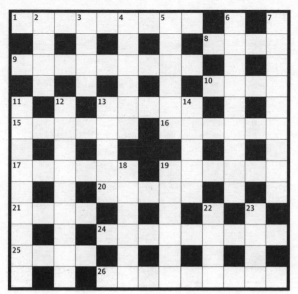

ACROSS

1 Kind of social scientist — weekly magazine (9)

8 Ireland, poetically (4)

9 Wheedle (5–4)

10 Move very gradually (4)

13 Over (5)

15 Chronological account of events in successive years (6)

16 Stormzy, for instance (6)

17 Fast-flowing section of river (6)

19 Directionless (6)

20 Listing (5)

21 Risqué (4)

24 Shabby (4–5)

25 Ruin (4)

26 Adaptable — relatives (anag) (9)

DOWN

2 Loose hood (4)

3 Never, poetically (4)

4 Morning worship (6)

5 Alloy used in bonding metals (6)

6 International motor sports event (5,4)

7 Religious recluse (9)

11 Importing that guarantees a more equitable deal for the producers (4,5)

12 An ___ Calls, 1945 Priestley play (9)

13 Avoid (5)

14 Dedicated follower of fashion (5)

18 Nap (6)

19 Spans (6)

22 Creator of the musical Oliver!, d. 1999 (4)

23 Untrustworthy person (4)

Solution see page 263

125

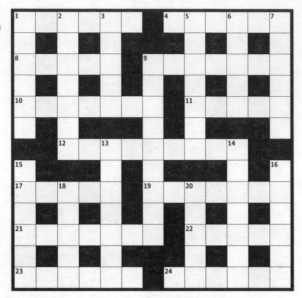

ACROSS

1 Polite — fitting (6)
4 Hired gun (3,3)
8 Language of ancient Rome (5)
9 Widow Twankey's son (7)
10 Pay each for oneself (2,5)
11 Small bay (5)
12 Involving a long period of time stretching into the future (4–5)
17 Strikes a golf ball (5)
19 Geeky (7)
21 Call together (7)
22 Type of computer disc (2-3)
23 Second childhood (6)
24 One of the Three Musketeers (6)

DOWN

1 Torrential rain (6)
2 Fortress — dialect (anag) (7)
3 Musical composition — tonne (anag) (5)
5 Language of modern Rome (7)
6 Replica (5)
7 XC (in ancient Rome) (6)
9 Sticking together (9)
13 Money kept in reserve (4,3)
14 Concise and witty remark (7)
15 Having gaps between (6)
16 The Apostle who initially doubted the Resurrection (6)
18 Doctrine held to be true (5)
20 Repeat (5)

Solution see page 264

126

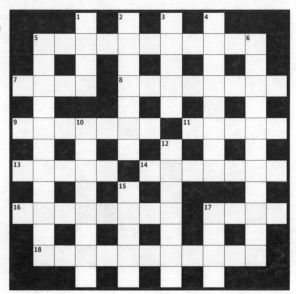

ACROSS

5 US state containing Mount Rushmore National Memorial (5,6)

7 Silent bad temper (4)

8 Broad-minded (8)

9 Heart and soul (7)

11 Proviso added to an agreement (5)

13 Extent (5)

14 Cigarette butts (3,4)

16 Lesson (8)

17 Effervescence (4)

18 Someone from Port of Spain in the West Indies (11)

DOWN

1 Ice hockey disc (4)

2 Cold confection (4,3)

3 Soil (5)

4 Appropriate for one's own use (8)

5 Walled indoor area for a racket and ball sport for two players (6,5)

6 Two a penny in the United States (1,4,1,5)

10 Intense elation (8)

12 Sack for letters (7)

15 US states that seceded from the Union in 1861 (5)

17 Turn over (4)

Solution see page 264

127

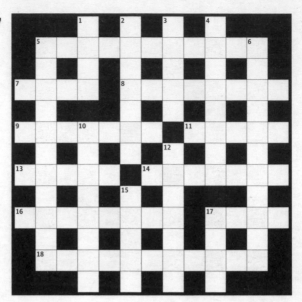

ACROSS

5 West African country — a UK Boris fan (anag) (7,4)
7 Very far from indifferent (4)
8 French wine region (8)
9 Solace (7)
11 Cooked in an oven (5)
13 Dairy product (5)
14 Independence (7)
16 Political troublemaker (8)
17 Facial expression (4)
18 Jumping-off point? (11)

DOWN

1 Boast (4)
2 Nut — left rib (anag) (7)
3 Get hitched (5)
4 Arrange in order (8)
5 West Sussex seaside resort (6,5)
6 First property square on a British Monopoly board (3,4,4)
10 Break (8)
12 Undress (7)
15 Pong (5)
17 Unauthorised disclosure (4)

Solution see page 264

128

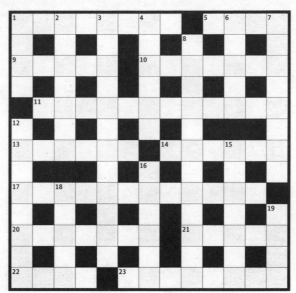

ACROSS

1 Retreat (8)
5 Grow weary (4)
9 Tourist island in the Bay of Naples (5)
10 Winding (7)
11 Bramley, say (7,5)
13 Period of time in office (6)
14 Trap-spinner (6)
17 Permanent (12)
20 Boost (7)
21 Mousy (5)
22 Lowest brass wind instrument (4)
23 Dressy clothing (4,4)

DOWN

1 Cord in a candle (4)
2 Proceeding from the general to the particular (3-4)
3 Being behind the wheel and under the influence (5-7)
4 Go with (6)
6 Respite (3-2)
7 Contraptions (8)
8 Thwarted (12)
12 Most stuffy (8)
15 Mid-meal (anag) — quandary (7)
16 Harrowing experience (6)
18 Addiction treatment (5)
19 Likelihood of something happening (4)

Solution see page 264

129

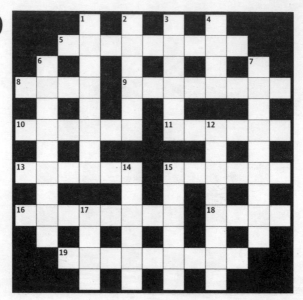

ACROSS

5 Hitting the hay (7,2)
8 Long walk in the mountains? (4)
9 Huge — bashing (8)
10 Write carelessly (6)
11 Punctuation mark (6)
13 Places to live (6)
15 Positive aspect of a situation (6)
16 Chary (8)
18 Bill of fare (4)
19 Able to predict events (9)

DOWN

1 New Zealand's largest city (8)
2 Put into place (6)
3 Sufficient (6)
4 Floppy (4)
6 Miscellaneous objects (4-1-4)
7 Insufficiently cooked (9)
12 Fine fabric made from goat's wool — sham pain (anag) (8)
14 What they speak in Liverpool? (6)
15 Not made explicit (6)
17 Open fruit pie (4)

Solution see page 265

130

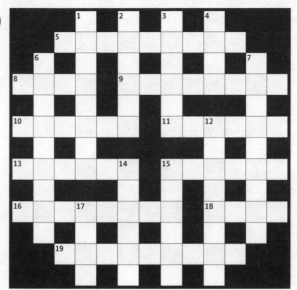

ACROSS

5 Woodworker (9)
8 Boundless (4)
9 Unmasking (8)
10 Shrink back in fear (6)
11 Late baroque style (6)
13 Repressed (4–2)
15 Swot for an exam (6)
16 Omit (5,3)
18 Ogle (4)
19 Follower of Jeremy Corbyn? (9)

DOWN

1 Strict disciplinarian — met train (anag) (8)
2 Formal discourse to an audience (6)
3 Concealed marksman (6)
4 In smaller quantity (4)
6 Keen-sighted (5–4)
7 Practical joker (9)
12 Courteousness (8)
14 Quantum of electromagnetic radiation (6)
15 Turning (6)
17 Calf meat (4)

Solution see page 265

131

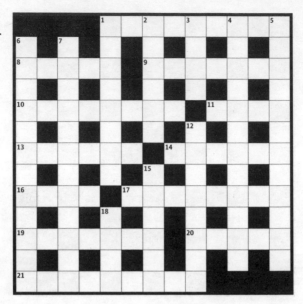

ACROSS

1 Do several things concurrently (9)

8 Deplete (3,2)

9 Blue or white cheese originally from Leicestershire (7)

10 Copied (8)

11 Unit of distance (4)

13 Mug (6)

14 Spice, mainly from Indonesia, made by grinding seeds of an evergreen tree (6)

16 River of the Yorkshire Dales (4)

17 Client (8)

19 Distended (7)

20 Lennox or Leibovitz? (5)

21 Unwilling (9)

DOWN

1 Cartographer (3-5)

2 Diminish (6)

3 Part of the eye (4)

4 Now (2,4,6)

5 Nursery school (12)

6 Crosser of the Rubicon, 49 BC (6,6)

7 Author of The Hunting of the Snark (5,7)

12 Take away (8)

15 Old gold coin, worth 21 shillings (6)

18 Group of countries acting together (4)

Solution see page 265

132

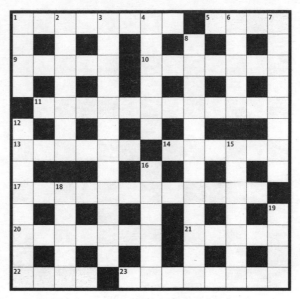

ACROSS

1 Rise as if by magic (8)
5 Pile (4)
9 Island south of Sicily (5)
10 International organisation concerned with human rights (7)
11 American national song, popular since the War of Independence (6,6)
13 Go back on one's word (6)
14 One discriminating against those who may be getting on? (6)
17 Julius Caesar's boast after his victory at the Battle of Zela (4,4,4)
20 Piled-up arrangement of hair on the head (7)
21 Seawater (5)
22 Protein-rich bean (4)
23 Plants, such as ivy (8)

DOWN

1 Acidic citrus fruit (4)
2 Bad guy (7)
3 American holiday on the fourth Thursday in November (12)
4 Go (6)
6 Alleviated (5)
7 Acts of defrayal (8)
8 Not to be excused (12)
12 Seriousness (8)
15 Slope (7)
16 One who revises another's writing (6)
18 Diaper (5)
19 Optical device using light to form images (4)

Solution see page 265

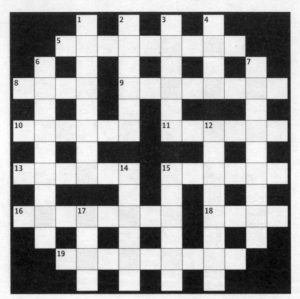

ACROSS

5 Tactless — to admiral (anag) (9)
8 Accomplishment (4)
9 It gets discounted fares for train travellers (8)
10 Take out a loan (6)
11 Castrated male (6)
13 Tropical fruit (6)
15 Grand — time of the year (6)
16 Literary gathering (4,4)
18 Slump (4)
19 Non-stop (9)

DOWN

1 Microbes (8)
2 Ancient burial mound (6)
3 Contusion (6)
4 Record (4)
6 It triggers a big bang (9)
7 On the dot (9)
12 Persistently irritating (8)
14 Dormant (6)
15 Leader of a religious community for women (6)
17 Generous — sort (4)

Solution see page 266

134

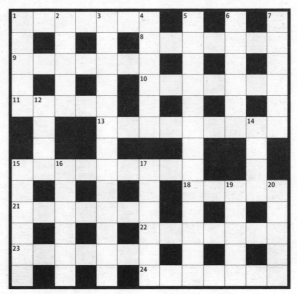

ACROSS

1 Gymnastic entertainer (7)

8 Heartfelt (7)

9 Substance from cassava used to thicken puddings (7)

10 Hand tool (7)

11 Charles Rolls's engineer partner Henry, d. 1933 (5)

13 With apprehension (9)

15 Dock worker (9)

18 Waterlogged (5)

21 (Person) uninterested in intellectual pursuits (7)

22 Flow (from) (7)

23 Involving fantastical imagery (7)

24 Equated (7)

DOWN

1 In pursuit of (5)

2 Response (5)

3 Overwhelmed by grief (6–7)

4 Riddle (6)

5 Work very hard (5,4,4)

6 Deceptive actions (6)

7 Oyster (anag) — level (6)

12 Remove and replace (4)

14 Organ providing oxygen to the blood (4)

15 Small amount of something liquid (6)

16 Regnal name of six kings of England (6)

17 Eric Arthur Blair (6)

19 Direction of fibres found in wood (5)

20 Surrender (5)

Solution see page 266

135

ACROSS

1 Fed up (7,3)
7 Full (7)
8 Explosion (5)
10 Ark builder (4)
11 Fast and furious (8)
13 Underpass (6)
15 Nun's headdress (6)
17 Investigation (8)
18 Suspicious (4)
21 Jewelled headdress (5)
22 Canadian province (7)
23 North American pit viper (10)

DOWN

1 Tea (informal) (5)
2 At any time (4)
3 Oloroso, say (6)
4 Suave (8)
5 American aircraft carrier (informal) (4-3)
6 Main revolving rod in a combustion engine (10)
9 Absolutely fine (informal) (7-3)
12 Miner's safety lighting (4,4)
14 Swagger (7)
16 Robustness (6)
19 Filled with enthusiasm (5)
20 Eyelid swelling (4)

Solution see page 266

136

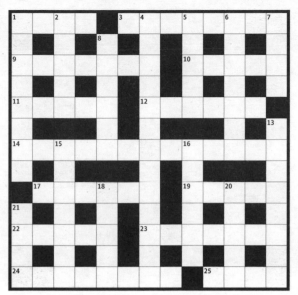

ACROSS

1 Religious song (4)
3 Trunks and bikinis (8)
9 Bacterium, for example (7)
10 Start — launch (5)
11 Terror (5)
12 Confine (6)
14 Prim and proper virtuous type (5,3,5)
17 Look up to (6)
19 Andean animal (5)
22 Another time (5)
23 Plantation of fruit trees (7)
24 Joy — eloquence (8)
25 Conference fruit? (4)

DOWN

1 First point of call on website (4,4)
2 Dry white Burgundy wine (5)
4 Always (Monday to Sunday) (4,2,4,3)
5 Connector for computer to telephone line (5)
6 Ban (7)
7 Customary observance (4)
8 Ticklish (6)
13 Inhabitant of Skye, say (8)
15 Strange (7)
16 Comfort (6)
18 Style of Greek column used for the British Museum and the US Capitol (5)
20 At speed (5)
21 Muscular back of the shank (4)

Solution see page 266

137

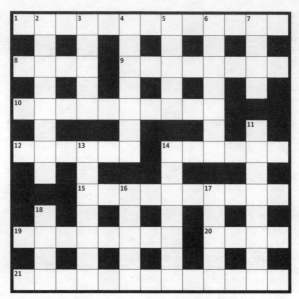

ACROSS

1 Miscellaneous articles needed for a specific activity (13)
8 Prevent (4)
9 Lineage (8)
10 Working (10)
12 Large fish-eating bird (6)
14 Tail bone (6)
15 Cites diner (anag) — tactless (10)
19 US Rocky Mountain state (8)
20 Unwanted hole allowing something to escape (4)
21 Decisive time (6,2,5)

DOWN

2 Philanthropy (8)
3 Savoury jelly (5)
4 By a stroke of luck (7)
5 French sculptor of The Kiss (5)
6 Saintly (7)
7 Listed entry (4)
11 Pigeonholed as an actor (8)
13 Horizontal underground plant stem — I'm her Oz (anag) (7)
14 Stop knitting — start sailing (4,3)
16 Gave out cards (5)
17 Head of state (5)
18 Flap (2-2)

Solution see page 267

138

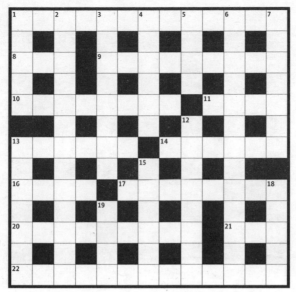

ACROSS

1 Take what's offered or get nothing at all (7,6)
8 Rocky hill (3)
9 Beef cut — net's odour (anag) (9)
10 Tavern (0)
11 Dwell (4)
13 With a submissive manner (6)
14 Nasty (6)
16 Desensitise (4)
17 Causing 18 (8)
20 Proviso (9)
21 French friend (3)
22 Distraught (6,7)

DOWN

1 Unforeseen obstacle (5)
2 Historic west Suffolk market town (4,2,7)
3 Honestly (anag) — surreptitiously (2,3,3)
4 Landed gent (6)
5 Go to the gallows (4)
6 Of an ambiguous nature (13)
7 Attempted (7)
12 Piffle (8)
13 Car for hire as a taxi (7)
15 Gambling establishment (6)
18 Heartache (5)
19 Bound (4)

Solution see page 267

139

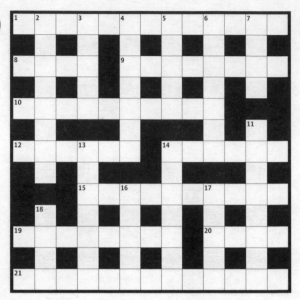

ACROSS

1 Hanky-panky (informal) (4,3,6)
8 OK! (4)
9 Seasickness (French) (3,2,3)
10 Eminent (10)
12 Letting (6)
14 Religious address (6)
15 Misdirect — seduce (4,6)
19 Light sledge (8)
20 Blooming — hopeful (4)
21 It will seem right eventually (3,3,3,4)

DOWN

2 Hung around (8)
3 Scrap (5)
4 Mathematical figure (7)
5 Available for hire (2,3)
6 Gorge — cheese (7)
7 Falsehoods (4)
11 Dark syrup extracted from sugar cane (8)
13 Reprimand (informal) (4,3)
14 Loyal (7)
16 Wrath (5)
17 Beat strongly (5)
18 Neither warm nor very cold (4)

Solution see page 267

140

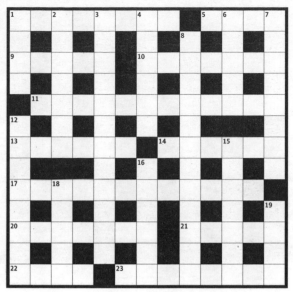

ACROSS

1 Most angry (8)
5 Begin to wake (4)
9 Excessive flattery (5)
10 Utmost (7)
11 Traditional (4–8)
13 Melt away (6)
14 Starchy food (6)
17 Laundry rack (7,5)
20 Freezing (in Alex?) (3–4)
21 Astound (5)
22 Prying (4)
23 Items not meant to be kept (8)

DOWN

1 Turning point (4)
2 Public address (7)
3 Extra educational session between academic years (6,6)
4 Character with a conventional significance (6)
6 Person with a stopwatch? (5)
7 Cures (8)
8 Outrageously expensive (12)
12 Action to remove an occupant (8)
15 Sickness (7)
16 Spent (4,2)
18 Takes the lid off (5)
19 Greek cheese (4)

Solution see page 267

141

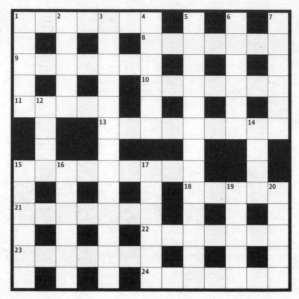

ACROSS

1 Its capital is Windhoek (7)
8 Bottle (7)
9 Cardinale, b. 1938 or Winkleman, b. 1972 (7)
10 Firmly embedded (4-3)
11 Japanese dish of cold rice balls (5)
13 Slender non-stinging insect with iridescent wings (9)
15 Game played on one's own ground (4,5)
18 Boredom (5)
21 Of part of the eye — reliant (anag) (7)
22 Singing popular songs to recorded music (7)
23 Degree-granting institution (7)
24 Cut open (7)

DOWN

1 Drinks straight from the bottle (informal) (5)
2 Method (5)
3 Doctor's ways? (7,6)
4 Former French colony, founded 1604, now part of Nova Scotia (6)
5 Alice in Wonderland's foul-tempered monarch (5,2,6)
6 Compact group of mountains (6)
7 Lookout (6)
12 Release (4)
14 Post usually occupied by another person (4)
15 Roman poet and satirist, d. 8 BC (6)
16 Spirit and resilience (6)
17 Spilled the beans (6)
19 Hangman's rope (5)
20 Awkward (5)

Solution see page 268

142

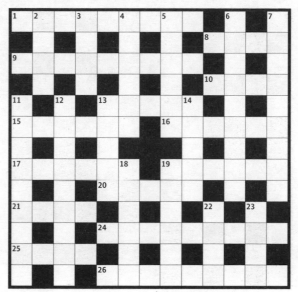

ACROSS

1 Tall garden flower (9)
8 Greek equivalent of Juno (4)
9 Iowa's largest city (3,6)
10 Objectives (4)
13 Affray (5)
15 Parrot (anag) — bird of prey (6)
16 Chemical element, Ra (6)
17 What mums and dads do (6)
19 Continuation (6)
20 Nocturnal mammal with a short flexible proboscis (5)
21 Central London entertainment area (4)
24 Possessing qualities of a man (9)
25 Porcine sound (4)
26 Author of The Wealth of Nations (4,5)

DOWN

2 Unlocked (4)
3 Source of illumination (4)
4 Young cow (6)
5 Smart (6)
6 Yummy (9)
7 Exact copy (9)
11 Small iron balls fired from a cannon (9)
12 Catch (9)
13 Increase (5)
14 Keen (5)
18 Herald's tunic (6)
19 Humorous TV programme (6)
22 In low spirits (4)
23 Link closely together (4)

Solution see page 268

143

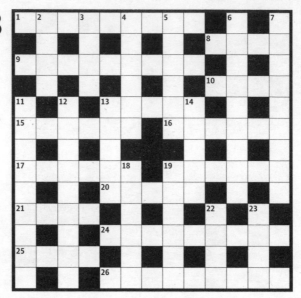

ACROSS

1 Made more obvious or prominent (4,5)
8 Replete (4)
9 Doctor (9)
10 Employer (4)
13 Hamper movement (5)
15 Unfounded rumour (6)
16 West Indian gangster (6)
17 Ski run (6)
19 Far from obvious (6)
20 Soak (5)
21 State of panic (4)
24 Relating to the sense of smell (9)
25 Frank — unsettled (4)
26 Fit as a fiddle (2,3,4)

DOWN

2 Small stream (4)
3 Care for (4)
4 Amity (6)
5 Annual Recording Academy award (6)
6 No longer valid (3,2,4)
7 Sloshed (9)
11 Events beyond human control (4,2,3)
12 Captivated (9)
13 X (5)
14 Hand over the money (3,2)
18 Taken unlawfully (6)
19 Celestial being (6)
22 Part of a procedure (4)
23 Cereal fibre (4)

Solution see page 268

144

ACROSS

1 Choose (6)
4 Lumberjack (6)
9 Fork-tailed bird (7)
10 Entangle (5)
11 Florida city (5)
12 Express eager enjoyment (7)
13 Elementary swimming stroke (5–6)
18 A risk-free risk? (4,3)
20 More rum? (5)
22 Twice (5)
23 Toy bears (7)
24 Bookkeeper's book (6)
25 Expression of surprise? (6)

DOWN

1 'Open ___ ' (Ali Baba) (6)
2 South American beast of burden (5)
3 Vocation (7)
5 Commencement (5)
6 Step by step (7)
7 Painter's tool (6)
8 Edible tropical tuber (5,6)
14 Offensively nonchalant (7)
15 Totally uncompromising (2-2-3)
16 Middle Eastern country (6)
17 Frolicsome (6)
19 Bout of overindulgence (5)
21 Training exercise (5)

Solution see page 268

145

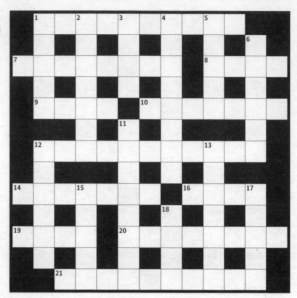

ACROSS

1 Kitchen appliance (10)
7 Minor inconvenience (4,4)
8 Notion (4)
9 Pretentiously cultured (4)
10 As an alternative (7)
12 Discreet (11)
14 Limp (7)
16 Declare solemnly (4)
19 Small pointed missile (4)
20 On the other side of the page (8)
21 Punctuation mark (10)

DOWN

1 River mouth (5)
2 Strew (7)
3 Sudden impulse (4)
4 Lincolnshire seaside resort (8)
5 Remove from a residence (5)
6 Old term for what is now Lebanon, Syria and Israel (6)
11 Giving off light (8)
12 Surrounding band (6)
13 Wrap right round (7)
15 Mutilate (3,2)
17 Use a loom (5)
18 Hardie or Starmer? (4)

Solution see page 269

146

ACROSS

1 V-shaped hairline point on the forehead (6,4)

7 Tube, the use of which may be banned during British droughts (8)

8 Ancient region of north-western European (4)

9 Jedi master of Obi-Wan Kenobi (4)

10 Relating to Russian rulers from Ivan the Terrible to Nicholas II (7)

12 Container for domestic electrical connections (8,3)

14 Society of distinguished scholars (7)

16 Cereal grain that's been germinated and kiln-dried and used in distilling (4)

19 Entice — bait (4)

20 Measure used in recipes (8)

21 Abrupt cessation of the taking of drugs (4,6)

DOWN

1 Tipsy (5)

2 Capital of Saxony (7)

3 Historical predecessor of Liberal (4)

4 Short mildly erotic film seen from a coin-operated booth (4,4)

5 Foreshadow (5)

6 East and West counties in England (6)

11 Broken down into constituent parts (8)

12 Lift (car) (4,2)

13 Member of a 1950s' and 1960s' youth subculture of nonconformism (7)

15 As a result of (3,2)

17 Honestly (5)

18 Not socially acceptable (to certain people) (3-1)

Solution see page 269

147

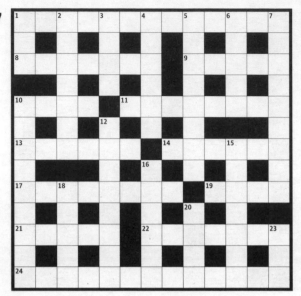

ACROSS

1 Best in its category (3,2,3,5)
8 Happy to wait (7)
9 Turn on a spot (5)
10 Retail outlet (4)
11 Tea (rhyming slang) (5,3)
13 Bring to justice (6)
14 Island group annexed by the US in 1898 (6)
17 Relating to a particular area (8)
19 Tarry awhile (4)
21 Unnerved (5)
22 President of the Russian Federation 1991–99 (7)
24 Questioned in great detail (5–8)

DOWN

1 Strike lightly (3)
2 Suppress (3,4)
3 Run away (4)
4 Meat and vegetable stew (from Lancashire?) (6)
5 Tit for tat (8)
6 New (5)
7 Furthest point (9)
10 Inducing sleep (9)
12 Virtually (2,4,2)
15 Craftsman (7)
16 It contains the vocal cords (6)
18 Gadget (5)
20 Run-down housing area (4)
23 Motion of assent (3)

Solution see page 269

148

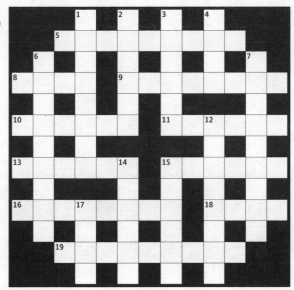

ACROSS

5 Displeasing to the eye (9)
8 Norse god of thunder (4)
9 Vilified (8)
10 Blacksmith's workplace (6)
11 Invent (4,2)
13 International cultural organisation (6)
15 Places for bowling (6)
16 Seaside resort in south-west France (8)
18 Very small (4)
19 Off-road motorcycle (5,4)

DOWN

1 Falsehoods (8)
2 Feeling of despair in the face of obstacles (6)
3 Jewish salutation (6)
4 Bullet — shot of liquor (4)
6 Small image (9)
7 On the way back (9)
12 Greek dish of lamb, baked on the bone (8)
14 Source (6)
15 Summerhouse (6)
17 Lightly cooked (4)

Solution see page 269

149

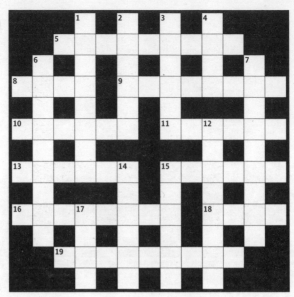

ACROSS

5 Exemplary character (4,5)
8 Ponder (4)
9 Gifted (8)
10 Obey (6)
11 Accumulated knowledge (6)
13 Person who eats and drinks far too much (6)
15 Evil intent (6)
16 Honourable (8)
18 Thin out (4)
19 Organised (anag) — overblown (9)

DOWN

1 Unsophisticated (8)
2 With a light touch (6)
3 Empty inside (6)
4 Low-fat (4)
6 Knee-jerk (9)
7 Bring together (9)
12 Faux pas (8)
14 Problematic (6)
15 Person unable to adapt to their circumstances (6)
17 Flag (4)

Solution see page 270

150

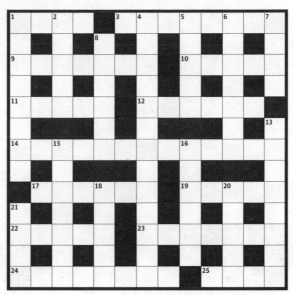

ACROSS

1 Misplaced (4)
3 Diverse (8)
9 Mocking irony (7)
10 Dickens' novel, ___ House (5)
11 System of reasoning (5)
12 Ill-advised (6)
14 Fruit — ever so Nigella! (anag) (7,6)
17 Russian chess world champion, 1975–85 (6)
19 One of the Queen's former favourite companions (5)
22 Roman god of the underworld (5)
23 Rift (7)
24 Make a positive impression (3,1,4)
25 Looked after (4)

DOWN

1 Depressed (8)
2 Body language of the shoulders (5)
4 Type of malicious software (8,5)
5 Joint (5)
6 Crime for which Lord Haw–Haw was hanged, 1946 (7)
7 It could contain soap or sponge (4)
8 Cry off (6)
13 Feeling remorse (8)
15 Structure carrying a railway or road in the air (7)
16 Cooking instructions (6)
18 Protruding from the surface (5)
20 What makes a woman blush! (5)
21 On this there is no guarantee of a profit (4)

Solution see page 270

151

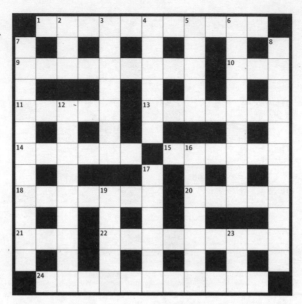

ACROSS

1 Blenheim Orange, for example (6,5)
9 Generally (2,3,4)
10 Farewell! (informal) (3)
11 Flash of reflected light (5)
13 Hold dear — he's rich (anag) (7)
14 Source of extreme provocation (3,3)
15 Cutting tool (6)
18 Special aptitudes (7)
20 Unit of length (5)
21 Hit a ball in a high arc (3)
22 Enrage (9)
24 Non-stop (11)

DOWN

2 Legislation (3)
3 Cold drink (4,3)
4 Look quickly at — cricket stroke (6)
5 Coppers (5)
6 Substance used to reduce friction (9)
7 Digital protection (11)
8 Unshaven (11)
12 Cannot be removed (9)
16 Bone (which sounds funny) (7)
17 Advantageous (6)
19 Talons (5)
23 Boring instrument (3)

Solution see page 270

152

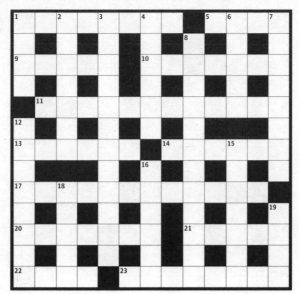

ACROSS

1 Drug used to treat shock — Ian moped (anag) (8)
5 Vulgar (4)
9 South American beaver-like rodent bred for its fur (5)
10 Display of bad temper (7)
11 On which ceramic items are thrown (7,5)
13 Defame (6)
14 Circle guarding something (6)
17 Extremely effective action (6,6)
20 Supplementary fortification (7)
21 Register (5)
22 Maintain (4)
23 Small tree with pear-shaped fruit — get Rambo (anag) (8)

DOWN

1 Out for nothing (4)
2 List of full-time employees (7)
3 Elevation at base of thumb (5,2,5)
4 Someone legally empowered to witness signatures etc (6)
6 High nest (5)
7 Dessert made by baking fruit wrapped in pastry (8)
8 Winter sport (12)
12 Hail Mary (3,5)
15 Rank of the highest British hereditary peer (7)
16 Parasitic fly that transmits sleeping sickness (6)
18 Grass-like plant (5)
19 Way out (4)

Solution see page 270

153

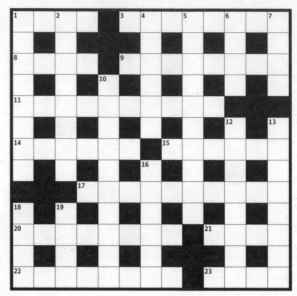

ACROSS

1 Covet (4)
3 Preachy (8)
8 Boy attendant (4)
9 Given to bragging (8)
11 Zest (10)
14 Actuate (3,3)
15 Small building with a wide view (6)
17 Mercurial (10)
20 Idle (8)
21 Paste made from fermented soya beans, used in Japanese cooking (4)
22 Container for leftovers? (5,3)
23 Gambit (4)

DOWN

1 Strong black coffee (8)
2 Lead a quiet life (8)
4 Emblematic (6)
5 Siestas can (anag) — help (10)
6 Upper-class gent (4)
7 Monastic accommodation (4)
10 It's often used in pies and canapés (4,6)
12 Lasting reminder (8)
13 Drudge (8)
16 Unimportant details (6)
18 Discovery (4)
19 Product of hunger (or guilt?) (4)

Solution see page 271

154

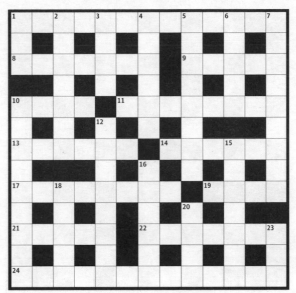

ACROSS

1 Essex resort with the longest pleasure pier in the world (8-2-3)

8 Wished for (7)

9 Miss Doolittle/s first name (5)

10 Edible shellfish (4)

11 Direct (8)

13 Alphabetic character (6)

14 Horticultural cover (6)

17 Over the moon (8)

19 Thin fog (4)

21 Hot dog topping (5)

22 Turn at batting (7)

24 (Of a garment) fitting closely (6-7)

DOWN

1 Blue (3)

2 Arriviste (7)

3 Parsley, sage, rosemary or thyme? (4)

4 Untidy (anag) — result of being in one's birthday suit (6)

5 Capable of being treated surgically (8)

6 English musician, b. 1951 — a sudden pain (5)

7 Flat (9)

10 Cancelled (6,3)

12 Advance fee – servant (8)

15 Wine from Tuscany (7)

16 Conclude (6)

18 Support for an injured arm (5)

20 Well protected or concealed (4)

23 Droop (3)

Solution see page 271

155

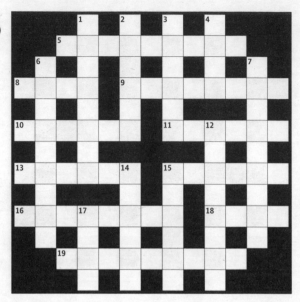

ACROSS

5 Verbal wrangling (4–5)
8 Sieve (4)
9 Easy target (4,4)
10 Edible stem of broccoli or cauliflower (6)
11 Pattern of coloured diamonds on a solid background (6)
13 Quickly (6)
15 Long cigar with blunt ends (6)
16 Fresh-faced (8)
18 Turkish monetary unit (4)
19 Fanatic (9)

DOWN

1 Fellow members of a male order (8)
2 I don't think so! (2,4)
3 Brazilian slum (6)
4 Eager (4)
6 Bright shade of red (6-3)
7 Heroism (9)
12 Stupid — germ loss (anag) (8)
14 Matthew Arnold's 'city of dreaming spires' (6)
15 Regular newspaper feature (6)
17 Metered vehicle (4)

Solution see page 271

156

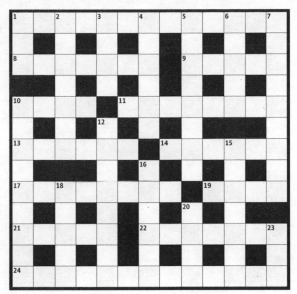

ACROSS

1 Is sexually attracted to (informal) (3,3,4,3)

8 Irish county (7)

9 Uncovered (5)

10 English spa founded by the Romans (4)

11 Brainy (8)

13 Punctilious (6)

14 Norwegian port city (6)

17 Takes against (8)

19 Struggle for breath (4)

21 Lenin (anag) — fabric (5)

22 Doubt — small weight (7)

24 Belittling words (13)

DOWN

1 Open trough for carrying bricks (3)

2 Statesman — treason (anag) (7)

3 Author of Les Misérables, d. 1885 (4)

4 Stopped (6)

5 Offered for payment (8)

6 Fraud (5)

7 Mars (3,6)

10 Confused (9)

12 Spanish landed estate — I had acne (anag) (8)

15 Lay hold of (7)

16 Professional female companion for Japanese men (6)

18 Air-filled cavity in the skull (5)

20 On the house (4)

23 Scoff (3)

Solution see page 271

157

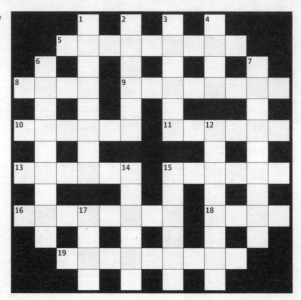

ACROSS

5 Thickening agent in cooking (9)
8 Sterile (4)
9 Delinquent (8)
10 Playful (6)
11 Gloomy (6)
13 Twitchy (2,4)
15 Purge (6)
16 Lethargy — not in CIA (anag) (8)
18 People (4)
19 Haphazard (3,2,4)

DOWN

1 Flute or oboe, for instance (8)
2 Seize — fragment (6)
3 Habitually (6)
4 Scottish island — mountains on the French–Swiss border (4)
6 Conspicuous (9)
7 Give up (9)
12 Henry VIII's warship that sank in the Solent (4,4)
14 Inventor with over 1,000 US patents to his name, d. 1931 (6)
15 Canal or hat? (6)
17 Copy without acknowledgement (4)

Solution see page 272

158

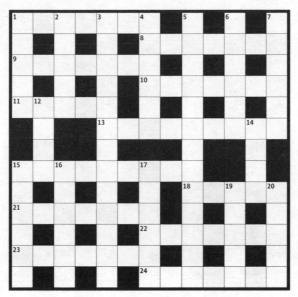

ACROSS

1 Fame (7)

8 Release (7)

9 Israeli collective farm (7)

10 Stringed instruments plucked when lying flat (7)

11 What powered old engines (5)

13 Artefacts distinctive of the US (9)

15 Student's holdall (9)

18 Particularly baffling problem (5)

21 Ray of light (7)

22 Protestant advocating total immersion at a christening (7)

23 Canadian cop on a horse? (7)

24 In the country manner (7)

DOWN

1 Followers of Guru Nanak (5)

2 Saunter (5)

3 Female baton twirler with a marching band (4,9)

4 Prevent from speaking out (6)

5 Ink soaker-upper (8,5)

6 Small shop in Spain selling wine and groceries (6)

7 Water parted by God to let Moses lead the Israelites out of Egypt (3,3)

12 Bathroom powder (4)

14 Leading resort on the French Riviera (4)

15 Seeds producing an edible oil (6)

16 Privilege (6)

17 Aircraft designed to drop high explosives (6)

19 Cause liquid to overflow (5)

20 Mole's friend in The Wind in the Willows (5)

Solution see page 272

159

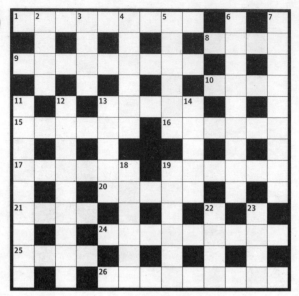

ACROSS

1 Clumsy (3–6)
8 Blood vessel (4)
9 Painting genre (5,4)
10 Broad (4)
13 Equals (5)
15 Get (6)
16 Bondage (6)
17 Aromatic spice (6)
19 Came to an end (6)
20 Largest city and once capital of Nigeria (5)
21 Try to find (4)
24 Small round thick beef fillet (9)
25 Fortitude and determination (4)
26 Staff (9)

DOWN

2 Stake (that may be upped?) (4)
3 People (4)
4 Bad-tempered and sulky (6)
5 Exertion (6)
6 Small coffee cup (9)
7 Entr'acte (9)
11 £ (5,4)
12 Figurine (9)
13 Digital image unit (5)
14 Footwear (5)
18 Aplenty (6)
19 Venomous tropical snakes (6)
22 Inert gas (4)
23 Hemispherical structure (4)

Solution see page 272

160

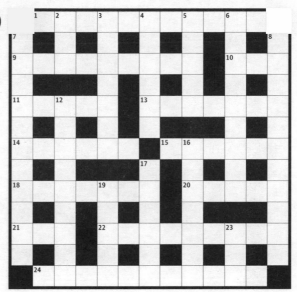

ACROSS

1 Book by Mary Shelley or Bram Stoker, for example (6,5)
9 Tender regard (9)
10 Self-importance (3)
11 Palestinian governing authority of the Gaza Strip since 2007 (5)
13 Worry (7)
14 North American capital (6)
15 Clever (6)
18 Chinese breed of dog (4-3)
20 Belief system (5)
21 Rower (3)
22 Habitual internet user — cut nearby (anag) (9)
24 Lewis Carroll's fictional feline (8,3)

DOWN

2 Not operational (3)
3 Hand-held metal cutter (7)
4 Cheerful (informal) (6)
5 Proprietor (5)
6 Responsible for carrying out agreed policies (9)
7 Catwalk exhibition (7,4)
8 Roy Rogers' footwear? (6,5)
12 Old venerable woman (9)
16 Bend back (7)
17 City formerly called Bombay (6)
19 Blood-sucking arachnids (5)
23 Heavy metal stove for cooking and heating (3)

Solution see page 272

161

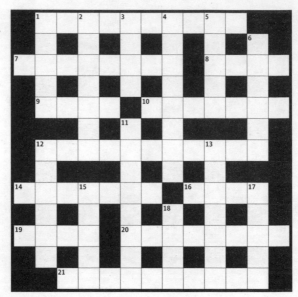

ACROSS

1 Coming together (10)
7 Small pile of soil blighting a lawn (4,4)
8 Legislative assembly (4)
9 Flat-bottomed boat propelled by pole (4)
10 Jockey's foot support (7)
12 Seamstress (11)
14 Mandible (7)
16 One attaching importance to social position (4)
19 Overabundance (4)
20 Inclined to believe (8)
21 All things considered (2,3,5)

DOWN

1 Munch noisily (5)
2 Person put up for a post (7)
3 Ages (4)
4 Splash out (2,2,4)
5 Rock bottom (5)
6 Homecoming (6)
11 Whale food (8)
12 Almost (6)
13 Huge (7)
15 Sandwich (5)
17 Human head (informal) (5)
18 Knitting stitch (4)

Solution see page 273

162

ACROSS

1 Teapot cover (4)
3 Lens maker (8)
9 Portable heater (7)
10 Permit (5)
11 Mindset of a group (5)
12 Get-up-and-go (6)
14 Without thinking (13)
17 Wall painting (6)
19 Acute (5)
22 Corny (5)
23 Rough (7)
24 Sums used to settle debts (8)
25 Restrain (from indulging in some pleasure) (4)

DOWN

1 Suspended mountain conveyance for passengers or freight (5,3)
2 Hoard (5)
4 One wants nothing but the best (13)
5 Mad (5)
6 Criminal (7)
7 Small amphibian (4)
8 Bite-sized Chinese dumplings (3,3)
13 Fellow-feeling (8)
15 Intimidate (7)
16 Cavalry commander killed at the Battle of the Little Bighorn, 1876 (6)
18 Leather with a napped surface (5)
20 Mindful (5)
21 Leave off (4)

Solution see page 273

163

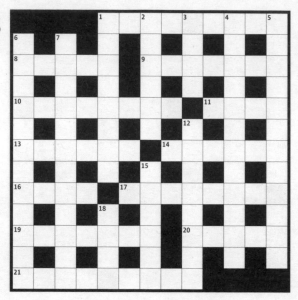

ACROSS

1 Perfect (4,5)
8 Eulogy (5)
9 Colourful decoration worn by supporters (7)
10 Divided skirt (8)
11 Curved masonry construction (4)
13 Appeal (6)
14 Old naval gun (6)
16 Cold and wet (4)
17 Read with difficulty (8)
19 Archbishop of York, for example (7)
20 Wooden projection shaped to fit in a mortise joint (5)
21 Dress for bed? (9)

DOWN

1 Crisis point when a critical choice must be made (8)
2 Overview (6)
3 Trick (4)
4 Emotionally sickening (3–9)
5 Comforter for an infant to bite on (8,4)
6 Immaculate (5,3,4)
7 End of flight without the wheels down (5,7)
12 Capital of Bermuda — musical (opened in New York, 2015) (8)
15 Person attracted to the opposite sex (abbr) (6)
18 Serve at table (4)

Solution see page 273

164

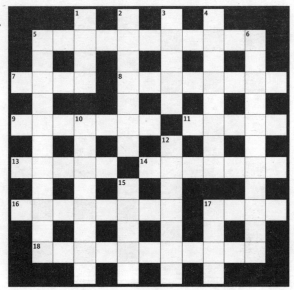

ACROSS

5 Heavy tracked earth-moving vehicle (11)
7 Nomadic inhabitant of northern Scandinavia (4)
8 A sincere (anag) — raise (8)
9 Quickly (2,5)
11 Cunning (5)
13 Large ladle (5)
14 Tropical grassland (7)
16 Find and bring back (8)
17 Bend (4)
18 Disturb the status quo (4,3,4)

DOWN

1 Gradation (4)
2 Umpire (7)
3 Pilfer (5)
4 Shout of praise to God (8)
5 Name for a rooster in fairy tales — nicer chalet (anag) (11)
6 Gloriously beautiful (11)
10 Lengthen in time (8)
12 Stratified (7)
15 Hated (anag) — expiry (5)
17 Dessert of puréed fruit and cream (4)

Solution see page 273

165

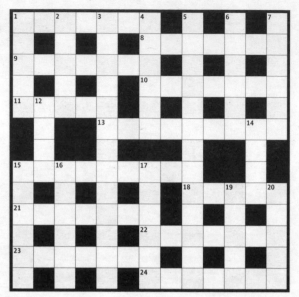

ACROSS

1 Form of flood defence (7)
8 So-so (7)
9 Graceful — refined (7)
10 Thrown out (7)
11 One-person canoe (5)
13 When one is fully grown (9)
15 Eleventh-hour (4-5)
18 Odds (5)
21 Grow coarse (7)
22 Turn aside (7)
23 Simon Peter or Judas Iscariot, say (7)
24 Plant stems growing along the ground (7)

DOWN

1 Tiny spot (5)
2 Hard up (5)
3 Clear-cut (5,3,5)
4 French cake (6)
5 State of bliss (7,6)
6 Signal for soldiers to return to quarters — it gets under your skin (6)
7 Devoted (6)
12 Patch (4)
14 Transparent (4)
15 Lasso (6)
16 Daze — shock (6)
17 Gentle — offer (6)
19 Sidestep (5)
20 They come in flights (5)

Solution see page 274

166

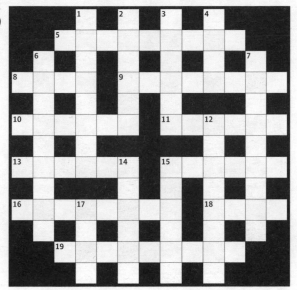

ACROSS

5 Tactic to gain an advantage (9)

8 Sunny — penalty (4)

9 Group meeting (to choose a pope?) (8)

10 Bird with no nest of its own (6)

11 Scottish dish (6)

13 Scamper (6)

15 (Succeed by) a narrow margin (6)

16 Standard post (8)

18 Island of the Inner Hebrides — think long and deeply (4)

19 Small puff pastry case with savoury filling (3-2-4)

DOWN

1 Nude runner (8)

2 Pampas cowboy (6)

3 Rocket journey's starting point (6)

4 Bridal face covering (4)

6 Tiny (9)

7 For use (9)

12 Serious eater (8)

14 16th-century freeholder of a small farm (6)

15 Part of a shirt (6)

17 Wax (4)

Solution see page 274

167

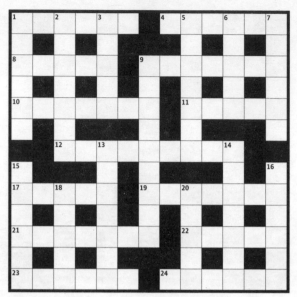

ACROSS

1 Provide (6)
4 Fraudulence (6)
8 Watery discharge from the nose (5)
9 Empires (anag) — assumption (7)
10 React in an offended manner (7)
11 Humiliate (5)
12 Someone who comes just for Saturday and Sunday (9)
17 Very long periods of time (5)
19 Early childhood (7)
21 Fielding position behind the batsman (4,3)
22 Terminate before completion (5)
23 Wolf-like (6)
24 Letters added at the front of a word (6)

DOWN

1 Flashing light instrument (6)
2 Screening before release for the general public (7)
3 Boundary (5)
5 Shade of green (7)
6 Heather — girl's name (5)
7 Ancient Greek or Egyptian city (6)
9 Going before (9)
13 Greek letter E (7)
14 Hang up (4,3)
15 Licit (6)
16 Grammatical structure in sentences (6)
18 Confess (3,2)
20 Stylishness (5)

Solution see page 274

168

ACROSS

1 Community of women (10)
7 Huge (8)
8 Mischievous children (4)
9 Sound of thunder (4)
10 Chic (7)
12 Interpret wrongly (11)
14 Shelf support (7)
16 Electrical SI unit named after a pioneering Italian physicist, d. 1827 (4)
19 Slender (4)
20 School holiday (4–4)
21 Off guard (10)

DOWN

1 Pry (5)
2 Citizens of Bratislava, say (7)
3 Simple (4)
4 Unable to manage independently (8)
5 Due (5)
6 Aquatic invertebrate — type of cake (6)
11 In conjunction (8)
12 Hard crystalline limestone used for sculptures (6)
13 Farmyard fowl (7)
15 Spice used in chilli and curry powder (5)
17 Weary (5)
18 Sound of thunder (4)

Solution see page 274

169

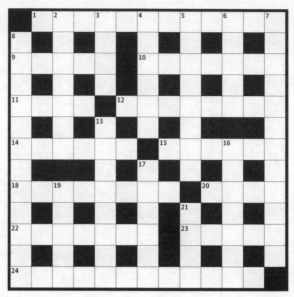

ACROSS

1 Large island part of Canada's most easterly province (12)

9 Large semi-aquatic pachyderm (abbr) (5)

10 Breed of cat (7)

11 Injure seriously, leaving permanent damage (4)

12 Gigantic statue that once stood at the Rhodes harbour entrance (8)

14 Not amenable to discipline (6)

15 French female chorus line dance (6)

18 Tea flavoured with bergamot (4,4)

20 Provide with money (4)

22 Warren residents (7)

23 Relative by marriage (2-3)

24 Chips to stand (anag) — game played with coins (5-3-4)

DOWN

2 Containing less (7)

3 Flat mass of floating ice (4)

4 Outcome (6)

5 Straight line on a slant (8)

6 Spaces covered by two-dimensional surfaces (5)

7 Severe scolding (8-4)

8 Agatha Christie play (3,9)

13 Slow-moving (8)

16 People with their partners (7)

17 Bible passage read during a church service (6)

19 Mechanical worker (5)

21 Decree — Italian car (4)

Solution see page 275

170

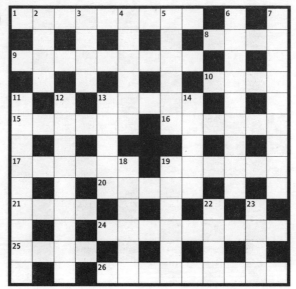

ACROSS

1 Unwavering (9)
8 Not bad (4)
9 Beekeepers (9)
10 Norse god of war, husband of Frigg (4)
13 Verdant (5)
15 Worthless (2,4)
16 Compelled (6)
17 Spectres (6)
19 Distant (6)
20 Bobbin (5)
21 Greek hero in the Trojan War (4)
24 Going for a song (4,5)
25 Unit of length (4)
26 Exclusion from a group (9)

DOWN

2 Misprint (4)
3 Pursuer of Moby Dick (4)
4 Thwarted (6)
5 Start on a journey (3,3)
6 Ratlike Australian marsupial — obtain cod (anag) (9)
7 Soldier — in red gear (anag) (9)
11 Mysterious (9)
12 Lack of knowledge (9)
13 Yobs (5)
14 Uncultured person (5)
18 Ill-gotten gains (6)
19 Dirty dog (informal) (6)
22 Smart (4)
23 Roman god of war, father of Romulus and Remus (4)

Solution see page 275

171

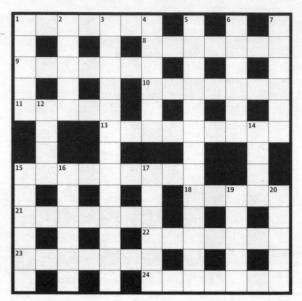

ACROSS

1 Natural environment (7)
8 Haematite, for example — Nero or I (anag) (4,3)
9 Absconds (7)
10 German castle (7)
11 Bewildered (2,3)
13 City serving Perth, Australia as its port (9)
15 Play ball (2-7)
18 Storehouse (5)
21 Smarter (7)
22 Enter forcibly (5,2)
23 Person from Birmingham (7)
24 Merit (7)

DOWN

1 Many-headed snake slain by Hercules (5)
2 Defensive players (5)
3 Repeatedly (4,5,4)
4 Disposable handkerchief (6)
5 These dashed on (anag) — impetuosity (3-10)
6 As well (2,4)
7 Tenant (6)
12 French-speaking West African country, capital Lomé (4)
14 Floor covering (abbr) (4)
15 Peevish (6)
16 Decide not to participate (3,3)
17 Inflatable mattress (3,3)
19 Fire iron (5)
20 Slight but perceptible amount (5)

Solution see page 275

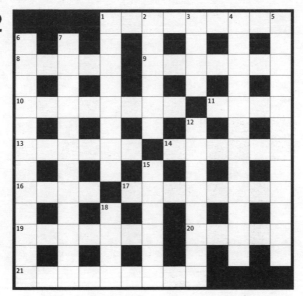

ACROSS

1 Alaska's most populous city (9)

8 Clatter (5)

9 Leader of several independence movements by Spain's South American colonies, d. 1830 (7)

10 Place where entry is dangerous or forbidden (2-2,4)

11 Bargain (4)

13 Stingy person (informal) (6)

14 Italian sausage (a kind of tactics?) (6)

16 Central London or Manhattan district (4)

17 Contrite (8)

19 Collection of public records (7)

20 Grieve (5)

21 Make aware (9)

DOWN

1 Prayer to the Virgin Mary (3,5)

2 Gave birth to little lions, perhaps (6)

3 Oleaginous (4)

4 Beneficial (12)

5 Painfully loud (3-9)

6 Without any doubt (3,2,7)

7 Relating to the facts of someone's life (12)

12 Charm that brings good luck? (8)

15 Misrepresentation (6)

18 Get-up-and-go (4)

Solution see page 275

173

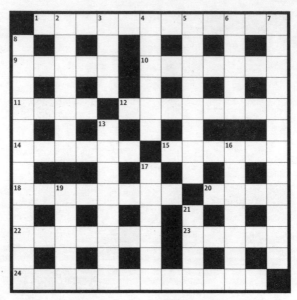

ACROSS

1 Brass tacks? (4,3,5)
9 Get cracking (5)
10 Place for comings and goings — or a trip (anag) (7)
11 Advantage (4)
12 Match officials (8)
14 On-screen control (6)
15 World's largest country (6)
18 Given back (8)
20 Charley's ___ , farce staged in London in 1892, revived and adapted ever since (4)
22 Put forward (7)
23 Get over (5)
24 Red fruit (12)

DOWN

2 Moral (7)
3 Protein-rich vegetable (4)
4 Spruce up (6)
5 Alfresco meal (8)
6 Vague — insecure (5)
7 Up to scratch (12)
8 Garden vehicles (12)
13 ___ Never Knows, 1966 Beatles song (8)
16 Put under pressure (7)
17 Department of France on the Bay of Biscay (6)
19 Less hazardous (5)
21 Blemish (4)

Solution see page 276

174

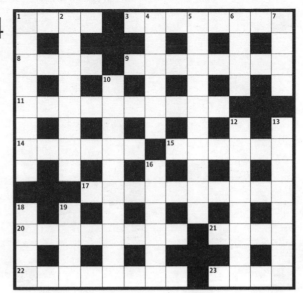

ACROSS

1 Farm building (4)
3 Martinet (8)
8 Obligation (4)
9 Reprimanded (8)
11 Go faster (10)
14 Duration (6)
15 On fire (6)
17 Totally in bits (10)
20 Consider comprehensively (8)
21 Riot (anag) (4)
22 In a careful manner (8)
23 Musical composition (4)

DOWN

1 Willing to obey (8)
2 Close-lipped (8)
4 Samovar (3,3)
5 Give in (10)
6 Unwilling to obey (4)
7 Ill-mannered (4)
10 Very popular (informal) (3,3,4)
12 Culturally delivered political propaganda — a top grip (anag) (8)
13 Scholarly (8)
16 Person totally subordinated by another (6)
18 Large pointed tooth (4)
19 Made up (a yarn) (4)

Solution see page 276

175

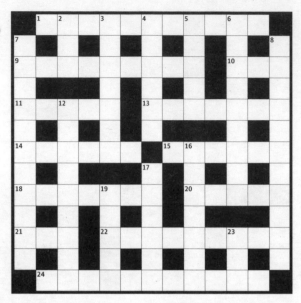

ACROSS

1 Landlocked Asian country (11)
9 Official in charge of finances (9)
10 Anger (3)
11 Reduce by 50% (5)
13 Eccentric (7)
14 Take in (6)
15 Spending time doing nothing (6)
18 Wild (7)
20 Person with legal title to something (5)
21 Name taken by 13 popes, the last dying in 1903 aged 93 (3)
22 Make a lot of trouble (5,4)
24 Regardless of what may have happened (2,3,6)

DOWN

2 Charge for professional services (3)
3 Female entertainer (7)
4 Very limited (6)
5 Tear to pieces (5)
6 Liveliness (9)
7 Quickly (2,3,6)
8 Aggressive (11)
12 Bedtime command (6,3)
16 Bishop's jurisdiction (7)
17 Hold in high regard (6)
19 Wall painting (5)
23 Do something (3)

Solution see page 276

176

ACROSS

1 Flying trumpeter (6,5)
9 Mesmerising person (9)
10 Chest supporter (3)
11 Overweening (5)
13 Turtle, for example (7)
14 Was jealous of (6)
15 Detachable spacecraft unit (6)
18 Spoilsport (7)
20 Stick passed in relay races (5)
21 Epoch (3)
22 Washed up pieces of tree (9)
24 Character (11)

DOWN

2 Software program (3)
3 Assistant to a priest (7)
4 Beehive collection (6)
5 Immediately available (2,3)
6 Nickname (9)
7 Dish of fried cutlets in breadcrumbs (from Ukraine?) (7,4)
8 Name of NASA's Florida site from 1963 to 1973 (4,7)
12 Procession of riders (9)
16 Going round (7)
17 From Damascus? (6)
19 Disloyal person (5)
23 Heading back to the pavilion? (3)

Solution see page 276

177

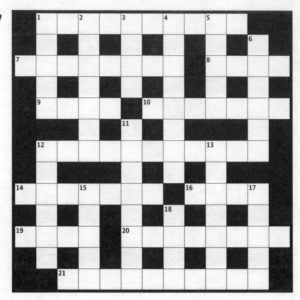

ACROSS

1 Occurring after death (10)
7 Source of government revenue (8)
8 Component (4)
9 Nymph who loved Narcissus (4)
10 Ceremonial staff (7)
12 Fitting (11)
14 Go before (7)
16 Fragment broken off (4)
19 Stitch (4)
20 One who worries others needlessly (8)
21 Bribe — a dark bench (anag) (10)

DOWN

1 Identify — station (5)
2 Road accident (5-2)
3 Frozen rain (4)
4 Cosmetic treatment (8)
5 Seize possession of (5)
6 Penetrate with a sharp instrument (6)
11 Refrain (4,4)
12 Respiratory tract (6)
13 Sorry (7)
15 Dance in a line (5)
17 Show-off (5)
18 Early 20th-century avant-garde art movement (4)

Solution see page 277

178

ACROSS

1 Person soliciting business without introduction (4–6)

7 Done by oneself alone (7)

8 Motorcycle — sulked (5)

10 The first murder victim? (4)

11 Best clothes (4,4)

13 Inform on — official statement (6)

15 Give one's consent (6)

17 Intentionally hidden (8)

18 Tramp (4)

21 Someone who lives on the labour of others (5)

22 Meat — in ovens (anag) (7)

23 Et cetera (3,3,4)

DOWN

1 Packing case (5)

2 Board game (4)

3 Treat in an indulgent way (6)

4 One who has become powerless (4,4)

5 Atone for (7)

6 Become beached (3,7)

9 Coming down (10)

12 Turn ripe (anag) — salacious (8)

14 Crushing remark (3–4)

16 Paris art gallery (6)

19 Pianist and composer (often associated with Brahms), d. 1886 (5)

20 On a single occasion (4)

Solution see page 277

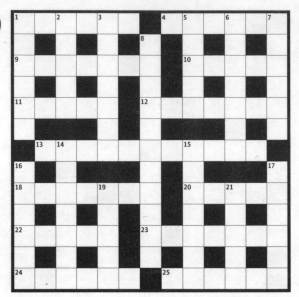

ACROSS

1 Reproach (6)
4 Bath powder (6)
9 Fix (7)
10 Metrical units with an unstressed and a stressed syllable (5)
11 Dagger symbols (††) used as reference marks in printed matter (5)
12 White crystalline sugar that comes in many forms (7)
13 Passed-along missive (5,6)
18 River running over the Victoria Falls (7)
20 Off-white colour (5)
22 Car race run over public roads (5)
23 Student with the same background as David Cameron and Boris Johnson (7)
24 Small fairy (6)
25 Wing added to a building (6)

DOWN

1 Think logically (6)
2 Push into (5)
3 Raft built by Thor Heyerdahl for his 1947 crossing of the Pacific (3-4)
5 Au revoir (5)
6 Fruit cooked or preserved in syrup (7)
7 Badly wounded (6)
8 Wild cat from the Indian subcontinent (6,5)
14 More modest (7)
15 Tropical cyclone in the Indian and Pacific Oceans (7)
16 Portuguese mid-Atlantic archipelago (6)
17 Flat rim on a wheel to keep it on a rail (6)
19 Land of the Pharaohs (5)

Solution see page 277

180

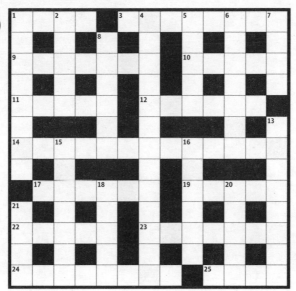

ACROSS

1 Destiny (4)
3 Defensive tower above a drawbridge (8)
9 Compartment suspended from an airship (7)
10 Flavoured milk drink (5)
11 Commerce (5)
12 Part of a BLT (6)
14 Piece of gymnastic apparatus (8,5)
17 Items of interest to a philatelist (6)
19 Wash with clean water (5)
22 Being that's apt to err? (5)
23 Unlawful (7)
24 Deride (8)
25 River crossing (4)

DOWN

1 One on the run (8)
2 Ringworm (5)
4 Stopped (2,1,10)
5 A close, affectionate and protective acceptance (5)
6 Prattle (7)
7 Want (4)
8 Gnawing mammal (6)
13 Beaten (8)
15 Not yet broken in (7)
16 Last Anglo-Saxon king of England (6)
18 Frenzied (5)
20 Small piece of tortilla with a topping (5)
21 Scorch (4)

Solution see page 277

181

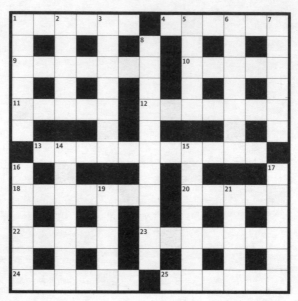

ACROSS

1 Of the most contemptible kind (6)
4 For free (6)
9 Navigation instrument (7)
10 South Pacific island country, gaining its independence from New Zealand in 1962 (5)
11 Bird's resting place (5)
12 Glowing with joy (7)
13 Very rich (7,2,2)
18 Train (7)
20 Figure out (5)
22 Person living voluntarily outside their own country (5)
23 Degrade (7)
24 Tried (6)
25 In repose (2,4)

DOWN

1 Official agreement (6)
2 Kind of jet (5)
3 Latchet (anag) — possession (7)
5 Flattened to the ground (5)
6 Kettledrums (7)
7 Roughly built hut (6)
8 Bitterness (11)
14 Sea creature with three hearts (7)
15 Examine closely (7)
16 Take into custody (6)
17 It ripens in a vine pod underground (6)
19 Saltpetre (5)
21 Retrogress (5)

Solution see page 278

182

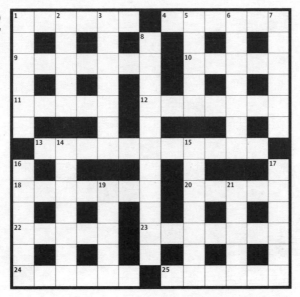

ACROSS

1 Epitomise (6)

4 Treeless plain of eastern Russia and Siberia (6)

9 (Musically) fast (7)

10 Clinically overweight (5)

11 Colour lightly (5)

12 Gift (informal) (7)

13 Green (3-8)

18 Move mouth to fit a soundtrack (3-4)

20 Bladed cleaner? (5)

22 Bee pack (5)

23 Eating away of rock, say (7)

24 How to produce patterned colour on cloth — eyed it (anag) (3-3)

25 Capital of North Macedonia (6)

DOWN

1 Nicely warm (6)

2 English actor — former US vice-presidential candidate (5)

3 Cover for something embarrassing (3,4)

5 Figure of speech (5)

6 Knot-shaped glazed and salted biscuit (7)

7 Cricket side? (6)

8 Source of food for the deprived (4,7)

14 Small iced confection in a paper case (7)

15 Chrysler Building city (3,4)

16 Secret — covert (6)

17 A founding member of the European Economic Community (6)

19 Delicious (informal) (5)

21 Groom carefully (5)

Solution see page 278

183

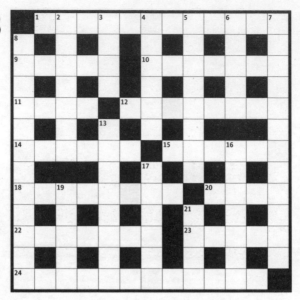

ACROSS

1 Incident attracting serious controversy (5,7)
9 Of the eye (5)
10 City buried in AD 79 by a volcanic eruption (7)
11 Hoodlum (4)
12 Earl's wife (8)
14 Alumnus (3,3)
15 Person moving sheep (6)
18 Celebration (8)
20 Exclude (4)
22 Ceremonially dressed (7)
23 Sharp pointed projection (5)
24 Pre-school institution for little children (12)

DOWN

2 Stagger (7)
3 Use lips and mouth to create a partial vacuum (4)
4 Jailer (6)
5 Leading light (8)
6 (In music) long note (5)
7 Plan for future disengagement from a commitment (4,8)
8 Person with a compulsion to be in charge (7,5)
13 Gregarious (8)
16 Go away (7)
17 Person effectively controlled by another (6)
19 Device making a loud wailing sound (5)
21 Sharp pointed projection (4)

Solution see page 278

184

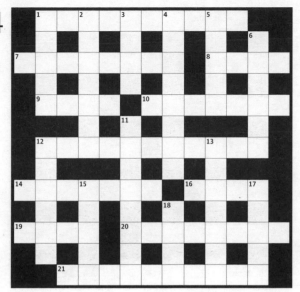

ACROSS

1 Resemblance (10)
7 Politically, an unsafe seat (8)
8 Kind of golf club (4)
9 Sex Pistols genre (4)
10 Below (7)
12 Best-selling product of its type (5,6)
14 Continue moving forward (5,2)
16 Advantage (4)
19 Smoke outlet (4)
20 Complete and undamaged — triangle (anag) (8)
21 Forbidden (10)

DOWN

1 Overwhelm completely (5)
2 Reddish purple (7)
3 Given temporarily (4)
4 Freed from anxiety (8)
5 Yours (archaic) (5)
6 Nose (slang) (6)
11 Rebuke (8)
12 Only just (6)
13 Great pleasure (7)
15 Absolute — diaphanous (5)
17 Sedate (5)
18 Small remaining piece (4)

Solution see page 278

185

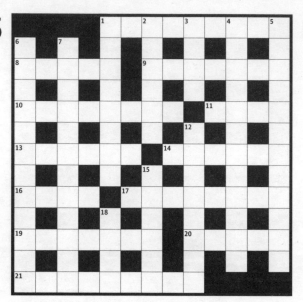

ACROSS

1 Painkiller (9)
8 Third most populous Japanese city (5)
9 Hercule Poirot's nationality (7)
10 Pacts (8)
11 Largest island of the Inner Hebrides (4)
13 Morbid fear (6)
14 Develop in such a way as to cause a problem (4,2)
16 Snug (4)
17 Don Quixote's region of Spain (2,6)
19 Young mares (7)
20 Birds that fly in a skein (5)
21 Final chess move (9)

DOWN

1 Building used for butchery (8)
2 Saunters (6)
3 Audacity (4)
4 Awkward situation (6,6)
5 Thought about (12)
6 Rodgers and Hammerstein musical (5,7)
7 French miss (12)
12 Geometric shape (eternal, maybe) (8)
15 Sickness (6)
18 Flower — colour (4)

Solution see page 279

186

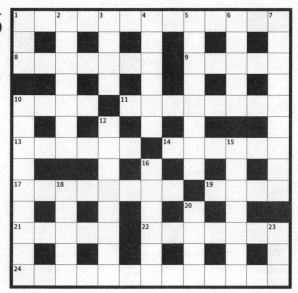

ACROSS

1 Trick played on a victim (9,4)
8 Braid (7)
9 V-shaped indentation (5)
10 Drag (4)
11 Message sent electronically to be delivered in written form (8)
13 Nub (of a nut?) (6)
14 Reflect (6)
17 Eyeshade (3,5)
19 Wickedness (4)
21 Go bad — confuse (5)
22 Threatening (7)
24 Government department (7,6)

DOWN

1 Drink — burst (3)
2 With sharp corners (7)
3 Soften (4)
4 Paid a brief visit (6)
5 Underwear or nightclothes (8)
6 Fish-eating mammal with webbed feet (5)
7 Fleeting (9)
10 Pole for an old infantry weapon (often said to be plain) (9)
12 Disease caused by lack of vitamin B1 (8)
15 Filled pasta (7)
16 Protective envelope (6)
18 Low point (5)
20 Squabble (4)
23 File a suit (3)

Solution see page 279

187

ACROSS

1 Bad-tempered person (10)
7 Flourish (7)
8 Son of Abraham, offered as a sacrifice to God (5)
10 ___ Bodies, Evelyn Waugh's 1930 novel (4)
11 Valued possession that's handed down (8)
13 Side roads (6)
15 Hostess in a kimono (6)
17 OK (3,5)
18 LSD (4)
21 Zany (5)
22 Walk wearily (7)
23 Observant (10)

DOWN

1 Shade of pink (5)
2 Bovine creatures (4)
3 Insectivorous plant (6)
4 Enclosures for birds (8)
5 Mountain-dwelling antelope (7)
6 On the level (5,5)
9 Take by force (10)
12 Slavic alphabet (8)
14 Greet (7)
16 Closely confined (4,2)
19 Get into trouble (3,2)
20 Green ornamental stone (4)

Solution see page 279

188

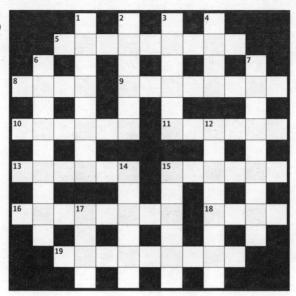

ACROSS

5 Clown in a diamond-patterned costume (9)
8 Member of an ancient Christian church in Egypt (4)
9 (Of a face) sprouting hair (8)
10 Slider over ice (6)
11 Felt hat with an indented crown (6)
13 Smoked ham (6)
15 Bob (6)
16 Ate greedily (8)
18 Under tension (4)
19 With a low neckline (9)

DOWN

1 Handyman (8)
2 Not so fast (6)
3 Force liquid out as a jet (6)
4 Exploit — white liquid (4)
6 Betting agent (9)
7 Ballet posture, on one leg (9)
12 Nettle (8)
14 Limited (6)
15 Prolonged affectionate embrace (6)
17 Heed (4)

Solution see page 279

189

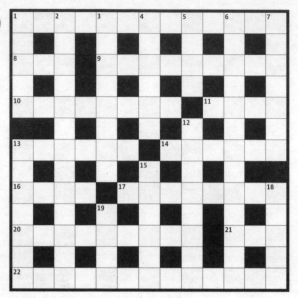

ACROSS

1 Astounded (13)
8 Cheat (3)
9 Aristocratic (9)
10 Get on (3,2,3)
11 Leading actor (4)
13 Offensively unpleasant odour (6)
14 Spoilt — bankrupt (6)
16 Very keen (4)
17 Totally non-aquatic turtle (8)
20 Journey there and back (5,4)
21 Old overworked horse (3)
22 Shrewd operator (7-6)

DOWN

1 What the rejected lover may carry? (5)
2 Topical (2-2-3-6)
3 Idiot (informal) (8)
4 Formally approve (6)
5 Double (4)
6 Not deliberate (13)
7 Related (7)
12 Umpteen (8)
13 House or tree bird (7)
15 Intense dislike (6)
18 Very keen (5)
19 Object of devotion (4)

Solution see page 280

190

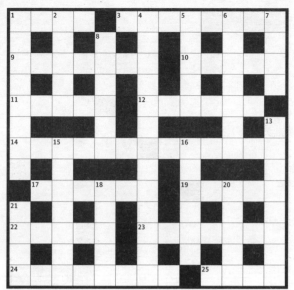

ACROSS

1 Protest — excitement (4)
3 Aerosol (5,3)
9 Defeat (7)
10 Express one's opinion openly (5)
11 Deposit — gatehouse (5)
12 What? (6)
14 Small biscuit containing a prediction (7,6)
17 Plum-coloured (6)
19 Overly self-confident (5)
22 Sheepish? (5)
23 Time off work? (7)
24 Rope-pulling team sport (3,2,3)
25 Ringer (4)

DOWN

1 Plastic surgery to reduce wrinkles (8)
2 Ecclesiastical assembly (5)
4 Items of gear (13)
5 (Illicit) sexual relationship (5)
6 Native American — helicopter (7)
7 Votes against (4)
8 Office (6)
13 Expression of (reluctant?) agreement (4,4)
15 One of the three Rs (7)
16 Unusually shaped, beautifully coloured flower (6)
18 Bundle (5)
20 Car with just two doors and two front seats (5)
21 Baptismal bowl (4)

Solution see page 280

191

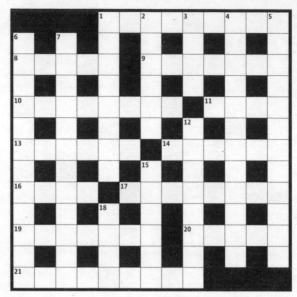

ACROSS

1 Say what you've got to say! (3,4,2)
8 Factory (5)
9 Coal miner (7)
10 In recent times (8)
11 ___ and gloom! (4)
13 Sea around Finland (6)
14 Unborn child (6)
16 Dark blue (4)
17 Quebec's most populous city (8)
19 Wishy-washy (7)
20 Become swollen (5)
21 Prime minister four times, d. 1898 (9)

DOWN

1 Broadcasting (2,3,3)
2 Equipment (6)
3 Skye, for example (4)
4 Alcoholic drink taken for a hangover (4,2,3,3)
5 Greek fish roe paste (12)
6 Enthralling (12)
7 Spanish farewell (5,2,5)
12 Designed to be carried (8)
15 Haitian witchcraft (6)
18 Imitates (4)

Solution see page 280

192

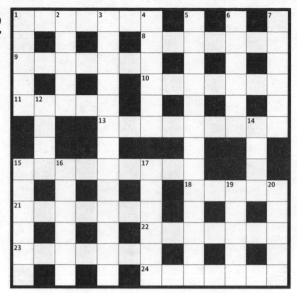

ACROSS

1 Violent attack (7)
8 Hoping for perfection? (7)
9 Feudal bondage (7)
10 Source of warmth on 5 November? (7)
11 Participate (5)
13 Inducement (informal) (9)
15 Home for parentless children (9)
18 Pals (5)
21 Bird of the crow family (7)
22 Feeling — sentiment (7)
23 Military rank (7)
24 Pristine (4,3)

DOWN

1 Part of a church, alongside the nave (5)
2 Bar or rod acting as a brace (5)
3 Comprehension (13)
4 Roll over and over (6)
5 All day and all night (5,3,5)
6 Immobilise (6)
7 Make attractive (6)
12 Close (4)
14 Scholastic test (abbr) (4)
15 Goal (6)
16 Predicament (6)
17 Also (2,4)
19 Marriage (5)
20 Tough cord connecting muscle to bone (5)

Solution see page 280

193

ACROSS

1 Bad luck! (4,6)
7 Turning point (7)
8 Let (5)
10 Little lake island (4)
11 Attractive (8)
13 Looking like a monkey (6)
15 Dealing with canines? (6)
17 Danger's over! (3-5)
18 English rock band, formed in 1988 (4)
21 Further (5)
22 Cigar-smoking Marx brother (7)
23 Naughtiness (5-5)

DOWN

1 Hi! (5)
2 Happening once in a blue moon (4)
3 Builder's powder (6)
4 Inspector (8)
5 Person playing alone (7)
6 Male toiletry (10)
9 Latitude (6,4)
12 Approximate (8)
14 Army reserves (7)
16 Slam in the slammer! (4,2)
19 Fortunate (5)
20 Grain (4)

Solution see page 281

194

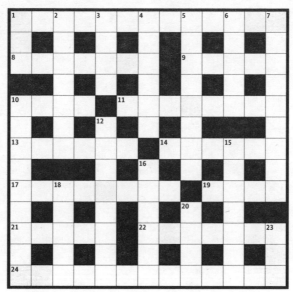

ACROSS

1 Grit sweeper on? (anag) — it makes driving easier (5,8)

8 Sincere — humourless (7)

9 Tree with orange-red berry-like fruits (5)

10 Peak (4)

11 Savaged (4,4)

13 Hergé's adventurous young Belgian reporter (6)

14 Put the ball in the net (6)

17 Branch of mathematics (8)

19 Substance taker (4)

21 Excuse (5)

22 Treating badly (7)

24 In a lackadaisical fashion (4-9)

DOWN

1 Fruit or meat dish (3)

2 Labourer (7)

3 Regrets (4)

4 Italian painter of the Venetian school, patronised by Philip II of Spain (6)

5 Wife of Orpheus (8)

6 From Des Moines? (5)

7 Explosive invented in 9th-century China (9)

10 Signature (9)

12 Accompaniment at mealtime (4,4)

15 Quash (7)

16 Misprints in a book (6)

18 Type of bay window (5)

20 Sculpture — ruined (4)

23 Writer of The Beggar's Opera (3)

Solution see page 281

195

ACROSS

1 Dabbler in the arts? (10)
7 Out of a hundred (3,4)
8 Direction — thorn (anag) (5)
10 International currency (4)
11 Infernal South African buzzer (8)
13 Clear (6)
15 Chesty (anag) — cut (6)
17 California city, setting for Steinbeck's Cannery Row (8)
18 Declines (4)
21 Message (from a bird?) (5)
22 Interpretation from a different viewpoint (7)
23 Neutral area between opponents (6,4)

DOWN

1 More desperate (5)
2 Art song for voice and piano (4)
3 I disapprove! (3-3)
4 Declare (8)
5 Woe (7)
6 How fast one may go, legally (5,5)
9 Providential (6-4)
12 Drink consumed after a meal (8)
14 Old cloak — tame Una (anag) (7)
16 Semi-aquatic rodent — work hard (6)
19 Newly-wed (5)
20 Liveliness (4)

Solution see page 281

196

ACROSS

1 Places offering hot drinks and snacks (6,5)

9 Accident caused by driver who doesn't stop (3-3-3)

10 Complete collection (3)

11 Happen time after time (5)

13 Less polluted (7)

14 Unchanging (6)

15 Place serving drink in France (6)

18 Artist's workshop (7)

20 Steep (5)

21 Fury (3)

22 Part of a bicycle tyre (5,4)

24 Petty (11)

DOWN

2 Decide (3)

3 Final rite of passage (7)

4 Add quality to (6)

5 Therefore (5)

6 Relating to the time after childbirth (9)

7 Captivating (11)

8 Pigeonholed (11)

12 One who adapts quickly to new environments (9)

16 Receive by genetic transmission (7)

17 Wild horse (liable to buck?) (6)

19 Turn of phrase (5)

23 Ode on a Grecian ___ (John Keats) (3)

Solution see page 281

197

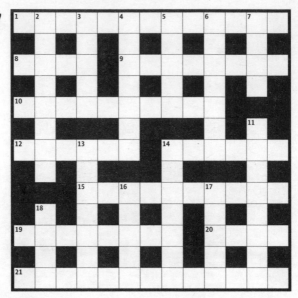

ACROSS

1 Finished completely and for ever (4,3,6)
8 Nought (4)
9 Maligned (8)
10 Structure hanging from the roof of a cave (10)
12 Baker Street detective (6)
14 Rudiments (6)
15 Bad dreams (10)
19 Have the idea for (8)
20 Publicise — stop (4)
21 Able to make plants grow well (5–8)

DOWN

2 Subatomic particle — enrol etc (anag) (8)
3 Salivate (5)
4 Beginners (7)
5 Spicy Pakistani cuisine with food cooked in a karahi (5)
6 Roof beams (7)
7 Ophthalmologist's speciality (4)
11 Timetable (8)
13 Eyeglass (7)
14 Bird that booms (7)
16 Intense sorrow (5)
17 Copious (5)
18 South African of Dutch ancestry (4)

Solution see page 282

198

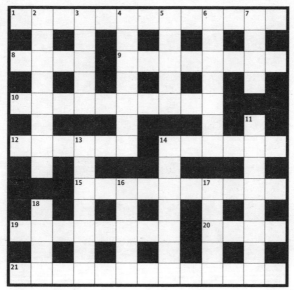

ACROSS

1 Parliamentary activity not marked by strong principles? (5,8)

8 Shoe ___ or family ___ (4)

9 Muddled (8)

10 Marked by strong principles (4-6)

12 Temporary fault (6)

14 Blurred (6)

15 Liquid added to car radiator (10)

19 Non-sexual (8)

20 Step up the ladder (4)

21 Mitt worn by fielders (8,5)

DOWN

2 Pellet firer (3,5)

3 Choppers (5)

4 Mischievous (7)

5 Marked with wrinkles (5)

6 Move along heavily (7)

7 Cook (4)

11 Soviet Union president, d. 1982 (8)

13 Hot sandwich (7)

14 Allowing for distant and near vision (7)

16 Polynesian monarchy, member of the Commonwealth (5)

17 Become a member (5)

18 Kind of seaweed (4)

Solution see page 282

199

ACROSS

1 Prime minister, 1937–40 (11)

9 Holiest fast day of the Jewish calendar (3,6)

10 Buddy (3)

11 Italian leader of the 1497 English expedition to the east coast of today's Canada (5)

13 Neat and tidy (7)

14 Moderate (6)

15 Freud's sex drive (6)

18 Atomic (7)

20 Fame — style (5)

21 Trumpland? (3)

22 Indirect expression used in place of an offensive one (9)

24 Aircraft's undercarriage (7,4)

DOWN

2 Finished edge of a piece of cloth (3)

3 Make damp (7)

4 Use (6)

5 Horrifying — sensational (5)

6 Unbiased (9)

7 With the same time period — shuns coy Ron (anag) (11)

8 Delay having to make a decision (4,3,4)

12 Close-fitting woollen head cover (9)

16 RMS Titanic's nemesis (7)

17 Come by (4,2)

19 Correct (5)

23 Princess in a Gilbert and Sullivan comic opera (3)

Solution see page 282

200

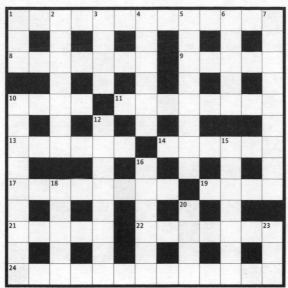

ACROSS

1 Very bad catcher (13)
8 Sundry (7)
9 General meaning (5)
10 Average result (4)
11 Class of university (3–5)
13 Very sad (6)
14 Opinions expressed in interviews with those in street (3,3)
17 Shy (8)
19 Very intimate get-together (4)
21 Greyish-green (5)
22 Claim brought to court (7)
24 In a very good position! (7,6)

DOWN

1 Try (3)
2 Small Greek restaurant (7)
3 Deserve (4)
4 Antenna (0)
5 Memo pad (8)
6 Weariness with life (5)
7 Money for those taking industrial action (6,3)
10 Very disreputable (9)
12 Queen Victoria's favourite prime minister, d. 1881 (8)
15 Patterned flooring made with wooden blocks (7)
16 Remove a blockage (6)
18 Rotate — dance (5)
20 Pitcher (4)
23 Doll or teddy, say (3)

Solution see page 282

201

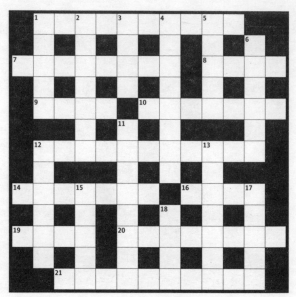

ACROSS

1 Dentures (5,5)
7 Rid (someone) of a mistaken idea (8)
8 No longer relevant (4)
9 Lean over (4)
10 Transgress (7)
12 The worse for wear? (11)
14 Molecular science applied to industrial processes (7)
16 Humanities (4)
19 Humble request (4)
20 Judicial assembly (8)
21 Dug in (10)

DOWN

1 Chat up (5)
2 Distribute small circulars (7)
3 Largest native Australian birds (4)
4 Lens(es) at the viewing end of an optical instrument (8)
5 Affected by changes in sea level (5)
6 Tangled into a mass (6)
11 Person nominated to carry out the terms of a will (8)
12 Spear-like shape formed by the freezing of dripping water (6)
13 By means of (7)
15 Exercise in preparation for an event (5)
17 Very conventional and dull (5)
18 Comportment (4)

Solution see page 283

202

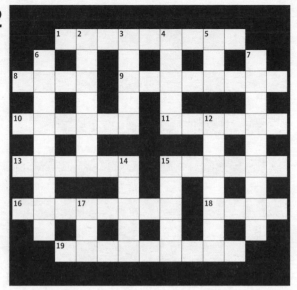

ACROSS

1 Send to Coventry (9)

8 French couturier, creator of the New Look in 1947 (4)

9 Impetus gained by a moving object (8)

10 Cease operating (3,3)

11 Dead body (6)

13 Change sides (6)

15 Monkey (6)

16 Last match in a knockout football competition (3,5)

18 Consequently (4)

19 Unpleasant conclusion (6,3)

DOWN

2 Dickens' miser (7)

3 Terms of reference (5)

4 Funny (5)

5 Star round which we orbit (3)

6 Calculate — fathom (6,3)

7 Bold in speech (9)

12 Remind someone of an embarrassment (3,2,2)

14 Restorative (5)

15 Intimidate (5)

17 Excess body weight (3)

Solution see page 283

203

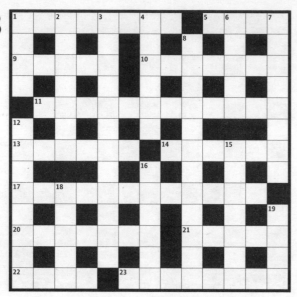

ACROSS

1 Innkeeper (8)
5 Laws (4)
9 Stretch of a river between bends (5)
10 Stare at closely (7)
11 Without integrity (12)
13 Prairie wolf (6)
14 Refresh the memory — on time (6)
17 Despite appearances there is still a chance of recovery (3,2,3,4)
20 Without any attempt at concealment (7)
21 Unconnected (5)
22 Stylish elegance (4)
23 Carte blanche (4,4)

DOWN

1 Remove the skin from (4)
2 Soft soap (7)
3 That's permanent or widely accepted (2,4,2,4)
4 Growing old (6)
6 Swimming stroke (5)
7 Firmness (8)
8 Restore normal heart contractions, with electric shock treatment (12)
12 Grope (for) — board game (8)
15 Knead (7)
16 Large decorative printed picture (6)
18 Woody climbing tropical plant — a nail (anag) (5)
19 Render unconscious (4)

Solution see page 283

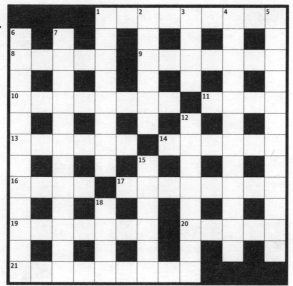

ACROSS

1 Being party to a crime (9)
8 Sharp vibrating sound (5)
9 Curious (7)
10 Wrote (8)
11 Written words (4)
13 Pre-decimal sixpenny piece (6)
14 Violently push — gist (6)
16 Senior manager (abbr) (4)
17 Platonic love between chaps (8)
19 Thug (7)
20 Little nocturnal bird (5)
21 Ironically witty remark (9)

DOWN

1 Nickname — eg non-com (anag) (8)
2 Early infantry firearm (6)
3 Folk myths (4)
4 As a result (12)
5 Normal eyesight (6-6)
6 Unexpectedly emerge as the outstanding performer (5,3,4)
7 Bloody-minded — non-UK car seat (anag) (12)
12 Irish national symbol (8)
15 Ukrainian peninsula (6)
18 International alliance (4)

Solution see page 283

205

ACROSS

1 Groundwork (10)
7 Stir up (7)
8 Correct (5)
10 Submissive — pedestrian (4)
11 Busy (8)
13 Locomotive (6)
15 Wanting food (6)
17 Eagerness (8)
18 Instrument played by Orpheus (4)
21 Plant material, used to make rubber (5)
22 Principal bullfighter (7)
23 Unjustly oppressive (10)

DOWN

1 Meeting place (5)
2 Second-hand (4)
3 Find — notice (6)
4 Not straightforward (8)
5 Current (7)
6 How Alf left (anag) — very unconventional (3,3,4)
9 Stuffed child's toys (named after President Theodore Roosevelt) (5,5)
12 Eating disorder (8)
14 Gruesome (7)
16 Male reproductive organ of a flower (6)
19 Sing like the Lonely Goatherd? (5)
20 Relating to ears (4)

Solution see page 284

206

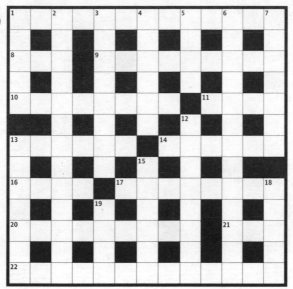

ACROSS

1 Not in! (13)
8 Misery (3)
9 Father figure (9)
10 Amazingly impressive (8)
11 Partition (4)
13 Weight on a fishing line (6)
14 Electric switch operated by pressing (6)
16 Moon around (4)
17 Forecast (8)
20 False addition to existing growth on the head (9)
21 Eggs (3)
22 Crunchy Chinese vegetable (5,8)

DOWN

1 Single (5)
2 (For water) 0°C (8,5)
3 Provider of a product (8)
4 Mean (6)
5 (Of film) bleak and cynical (4)
6 Make appeals that will never be met (4,2,3,4)
7 Level or rank in a group (7)
12 Crush (8)
13 In a way not yet specified (7)
15 Back end of a gun barrel (6)
18 Fungus able to convert sugar into alcohol (5)
19 Box without punching hard (4)

Solution see page 284

207

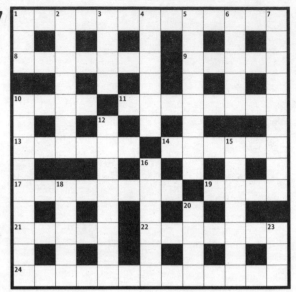

ACROSS

1 Taking unprincipled advantage for personal benefit (13)
8 Small bunch of long grass (7)
9 Enfranchised person (5)
10 Break suddenly (4)
11 Judge again (8)
13 Largest US state (6)
14 Metal, Cu (6)
17 Being in favour of policies to promote public welfare? (4-4)
19 Extract (4)
21 More (5)
22 Unweaned female sheep (3,4)
24 French mathematician and philosopher — screened tears (anag) (4,9)

DOWN

1 Frequently (3)
2 Thick tomato paste used in Italian cuisine (7)
3 Black bird (4)
4 Maintenance (6)
5 Person putting money up in hope of profit (8)
6 Book name (5)
7 (Move in a) spiral (9)
10 Trivial matter (5,4)
12 Horse with patches of white and another colour (not black) (8)
15 Cold dessert of fruit with whipped eggs and cream (7)
16 Historic city in the Loire Valley — incenses (6)
18 Be compatible (3,2)
20 Sixth letter of the Greek alphabet (4)
23 (Musically) to be played twice (3)

Solution see page 284

208

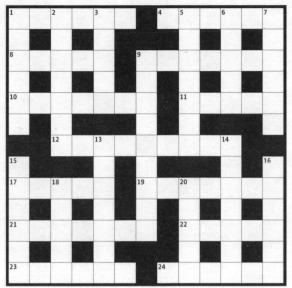

ACROSS

1,4 Stop just talking and get to the point (3,3,6)

8 Without qualification (5)

9 Taken up (7)

10 Suffering (7)

11 Offspring (5)

12 Morally corrupt (9)

17 Commend (5)

19 What's frequently found by a brush — stand up (anag) (7)

21 Urbane (7)

22 Pic (abbr) (5)

23,24 Official residence of the French president (6,6)

DOWN

1 Woos — legal tribunals (6)

2 Coached (7)

3 Throng (5)

5 Do away with (7)

6 Birds — toys (5)

7 Whirlpools (6)

9 Greatly surprised (9)

13 Scale for weighing (7)

14 Document conferring a qualification (7)

15 Expression of dismay (4,2)

16 No matter who (6)

18 With bunches of hair, say (5)

20 Brown tone associated with old photographs (5)

Solution see page 284

209

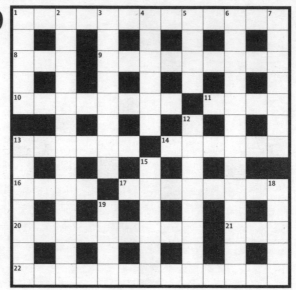

ACROSS

1 Rockabilly star depicted in the 1989 film Great Balls of Fire, b. 1935 (5,3,5)

8 Egg of a head louse (3)

9 Lost cause (anag) — French dish (9)

10 Variable-sized hole in a camera (8)

11 In good health (4)

13 Flemish artist, given to painting women, d. 1640 (6)

14 City near Leipzig where the 1919–33 German constitution was adopted (6)

16 Lima's country (4)

17 Presented together (2-6)

20 Overjoyed (9)

21 Female bird (3)

22 Taking joy from another's misfortune (13)

DOWN

1 Group taking power by force (5)

2 Parliamentary constituency before the 1832 Reform Act controlled by a family or tiny group of voters (6,7)

3 Cruising or racing in sailing boats (8)

4 Check — see to it (6)

5 Plunder (4)

6 Actor starring in The Odd Couple, d. 2000 (6,7)

7 Colonist (7)

12 Journalist (8)

13 Straight two-edged swords with narrow blades (7)

15 Kingdom (6)

18 Italian poet, author of Divine Comedy, d. 1321 (5)

19 Unite intimately (4)

Solution see page 285

210

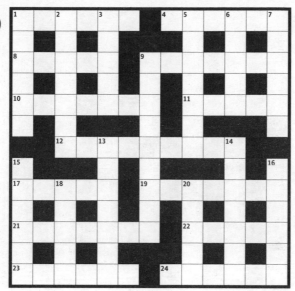

ACROSS

1 Front of a building (6)
4 Maintain (6)
8 Express great joy (5)
9 Simple songs (7)
10 Attire (7)
11 Author of The Iliad (5)
12 Yeoman warder of the Tower of London (9)
17 Seraglio (5)
19 Speech defect (7)
21 Amused (7)
22 Provided (5)
23 Allowing liquid or gas to pass (6)
24 Positively charged conductors (6)

DOWN

1 Savage (6)
2 Unit of electric charge (7)
3 Get rid of (5)
5 Attempt to hit an easy target (7)
6 Narcotic derived from poppies (5)
7 Wish (6)
9 Scattered (9)
13 ___ Harris, US country singer, b. 1947 (7)
14 Taken away (7)
15 Stop speaking (4,2)
16 Tines (6)
18 Happen again (5)
20 Inert gas (5)

Solution see page 285

211

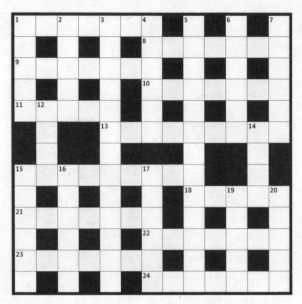

ACROSS

1 Abraded (7)
8 Love affair (7)
9 Cradle song (7)
10 Modern Persian language (7)
11 Protective garment (5)
13 Dreary (9)
15 Maritime paintings (9)
18 Slender graceful female (5)
21 Capricious (7)
22 Informal shindig (with Mother Brown?) (5-2)
23 Elastic (anag) — region of Spain (7)
24 City in Michigan nicknamed Motown (7)

DOWN

1 System for teaching singing (3-2)
2 Monarch (5)
3 Seafood starter (5,8)
4 Solid carbon dioxide (3,3)
5 Financial difficulty — abundance (13)
6 Whole (6)
7 Game (where love is nought?) (6)
12 Old weapon — Dad's Army character (4)
14 Speak in a sharp angry tone (4)
15 Rough drawing (6)
16 Over — not down! (6)
17 Chosen (6)
19 Lariat (5)
20 Skedaddle! (3,2)

Solution see page 285

212

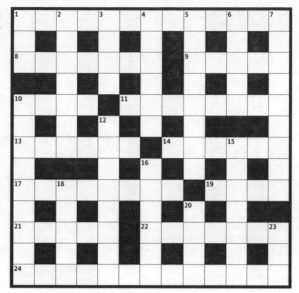

ACROSS

1 Roman official who allowed Jesus' crucifixion (7,6)

8 Perform better than competing retailers (7)

9 Inundation (5)

10 Bogus (4)

11 More expensive (8)

13 Away from the coast (6)

14 'The Godfather'? (6)

17 Southernmost point of Chile (4,4)

19 Cob or pen (4)

21 Scent (5)

22 Plant with clover-like leaves (7)

24 Document storage unit (6,7)

DOWN

1 In favour of (3)

2 After this, you get to serve again (3,4)

3 Two people widely seen as one? (4)

4 Fish (often smoked) (6)

5 From now onwards (2,6)

6 Garlicky mayonnaise (5)

7 Bedcover (9)

10 Stop paying attention (6,3)

12 Escaping arrest (2,3,3)

15 Heavenly crescent (3,4)

16 Polar region (6)

18 Move in a predatory way (5)

20 British Broadcasting Corporation (popularly) (4)

23 Auction item (3)

Solution see page 285

213

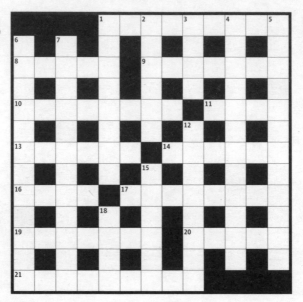

ACROSS

1 World War II flying bomb (V-1) (9)
8 School principals (5)
9 North African country (7)
10 Raised (8)
11 Supreme god of ancient Greece (4)
13 David Bowie's Space ___ (6)
14 Turf accountant (6)
16 Rescue (4)
17 Flee (4,4)
19 Parent's sisters (informal) (7)
20 Displayed (5)
21 Proscribed (9)

DOWN

1 Antipathy (8)
2 Stableman at a coaching inn (6)
3 Protracted (4)
4 Silent film comedy star, d. 1966 (6,6)
5 Unacknowledged barrier to career advancement (5,7)
6 Senior officer's principal aide and confidant (5,2,5)
7 Dowser, traditionally using a forked stick (5,7)
12 Funny business (6-2)
15 Cared for (6)
18 Audio equipment (2-2)

Solution see page 286

214

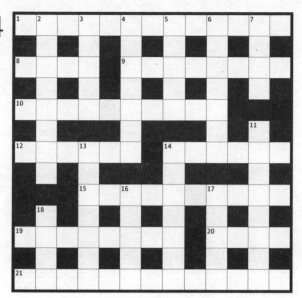

ACROSS

1 One who creates dance routines (13)
8 Paint crudely (4)
9 A poisonous halogen gas (8)
10 Child's game played with string (4,6)
12 Savvy (6)
14 Kick the football between an opponent's legs (6)
15 Slanderous (10)
19 Railway passenger coach (8)
20 Fashion (4)
21 No longer of the slightest use (2,4,2,1,4)

DOWN

2 Indian chieftain, subject of a Longfellow poem (8)
3 Pictorial teaser (5)
4 Made available (7)
5 Circular (5)
6 Flawless (7)
7 Fish-eating eagle (4)
11 Lowered in quality (8)
13 Sanction — red nose (anag) (7)
14 Old Testament book — narcotics? (7)
16 Fiddle (5)
17 Nervous (5)
18 Hangs back (4)

Solution see page 286

215

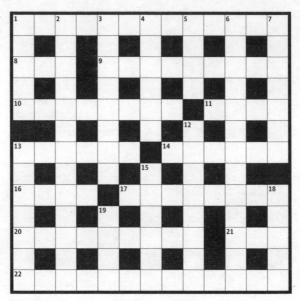

ACROSS

1 Celebrity (9,4)
8 Fake — failure (3)
9 Go in search of fun (9)
10 Intense study (8)
11 Clarified butter, used in Indian cookery (4)
13 Communal (6)
14 Test (3,3)
16 Public open space (4)
17 Kitchen deputy (4-4)
20 Pain relief (9)
21 A life (abbr) (3)
22 Brief personal encounter — single performance (3-5,5)

DOWN

1 Greek underworld (5)
2 Landing gear (13)
3 Age when one may legally buy alcohol in the UK (8)
4 Over the web (6)
5 Stage (4)
6 Miss Muffet's complaint? (13)
7 Beseech (7)
12 Commit a sin — spa's rest (anag) (8)
13 Singer who aims high (7)
15 Beetroot soup (6)
18 Overwhelming amount (5)
19 Unattractive-sounding fruit (4)

Solution see page 286

216

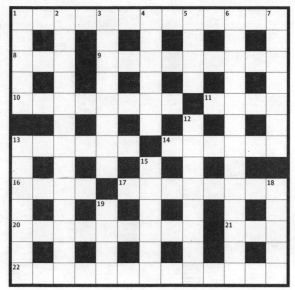

ACROSS

1 Madly (in love)? (4,4,5)
8 Wet soft earth (3)
9 East Midlands city, home of the National Space Centre (9)
10 Go faster! (4,2,2)
11 Let out (4)
13 Mollycoddle (6)
14 Cheats (anag) — small porous bag (6)
16 Communal bedroom (abbr) (4)
17 Toys made of cloth, stuffed and painted (3,5)
20 Gilbert and Sullivan operetta (3,6)
21 Perceive (3)
22 She was Duchess of Windsor, 1937–1986 (6,7)

DOWN

1 Songs of praise (5)
2 Poet who wrote To His Coy Mistress (6,7)
3 Witness (0)
4 Magical potion (6)
5 Gardening tools (4)
6 Issue or accept a challenge — lent tee shirts (anag) (5,3,5)
7 Snake — old wind instrument (7)
12 Officers' mess on a warship (8)
13 North Cornish resort with an annual 'Obby 'Oss festival (7)
15 Pester persistently (6)
18 Back of a boat (5)
19 Someone from New Zealand? (4)

Solution see page 286

217

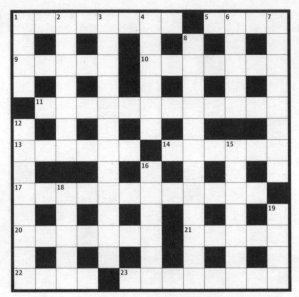

ACROSS

1 Precious (8)
5 Militant socialist (informal) (4)
9 Conserved (5)
10 Heraldic creature (7)
11 Misery (12)
13 (Of information) very recently received (3-3)
14 Annoy — provoke (6)
17 Person one knows, but not a close friend (12)
20 One of these does not make a summer (7)
21 Actions (5)
22 Badger's residence (4)
23 Amicable (8)

DOWN

1 Immense (4)
2 Prised (7)
3 Furthermore (12)
4 Raffish (6)
6 River running through the city of Arles (5)
7 Chemical element, W (8)
8 Trivial nonsense (6-6)
12 American river and state (8)
15 Ordained (7)
16 Reply (6)
18 Liquid measure (5)
19 Children's guessing game (1-3)

Solution see page 287

218

ACROSS

1 Copy illegally (6)
4 Abnormally swollen (5)
7 Bring to mind (6)
8 Artillery piece (6)
9 Traditional Indian women's dress (4)
10 Forwarding to an appropriate agency (8)
12 Round the clock (3,3,5)
17 Smoke and mirrors? (8)
19 Tack (4)
20 Option (6)
21 Revolving cylinder (6)
22 Launches (5)
23 Against (6)

DOWN

1 Marked in two different colours (7)
2 Without difficulty or delay (7)
3 Willingness to accept the behaviour of others (9)
4 Business (5)
5 Sovereign (7)
6 Small wooded hollow (6)
11 Not emotionally involved (5-4)
13 Composed of animal fat (7)
14 Maggots used as bait (7)
15 Muscle of the upper arm (7)
16 Fine plaster for ornamenting walls etc (6)
18 Thrills (5)

Solution see page 287

219

ACROSS

1 Dwell (6)
4 Cornered (2,3)
7 Thrown weapons (6)
8 Stringed instrument (6)
9 Profit-sharing enterprise (abbr) (2-2)
10 Polite apology (6,2)
12 Leading contestant (5,6)
17 Advance by jumping over the opposition (8)
19 Boxing contest (4)
20 Ascending — sort of struggle (6)
21 Animal fat used in making soap (6)
22 Be evasive (5)
23 Population count (6)

DOWN

1 Censure (7)
2 Cleaner for locks (7)
3 Nonconformist (9)
4 Farewell (5)
5 Have faith (7)
6 Distant, but within sight (6)
11 Small marrow (9)
13 Arrived at (7)
14 Bites off small pieces (7)
15 Harshly loud (7)
16 Investigator (informal) (6)
18 Untrue (5)

Solution see page 287

220

ACROSS

1 Sympathy for another's suffering (10)
7 Unfurl (4,3)
8 Dee, Exe or Wye, say (5)
10 London cricket ground (4)
11 Predict (8)
13 Frail (6)
15 Excessive severity (6)
17 Lively drinking party (8)
18 French military cap (4)
21 Brand of fine English porcelain (5)
22 Backache (7)
23 Circuitous (10)

DOWN

1 Foam on top of an espresso (5)
2 Upland tract (4)
3 Dress (6)
4 Angelic (8)
5 White wine from Umbria (7)
6 Break up entirely (2,2,6)
9 Only the Lonely was his 1961 hit (3,7)
12 Miss in German (8)
14 (Musical instruction) with force and energy — Rio's UFO (anag) (7)
16 Spanish rice dish (6)
19 Raise in rank or status (5)
20 What's fired from a gun (abbr) (4)

Solution see page 287

221

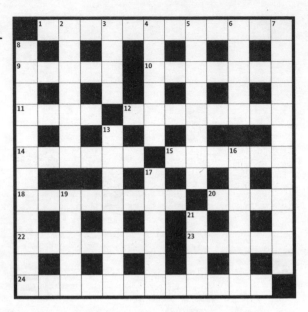

ACROSS

1 Musically arranged (12)
9 Part of a step (5)
10 Decisive (7)
11 River (which is originally blue and white) (4)
12 Muddled (6,2)
14 Shallow trench made by a plough (6)
15 Expressed (6)
18 Suspenseful (8)
20 Worry unnecessarily (4)
22 Liberate (7)
23 Winged insect — amigo (anag) (5)
24 Agent that destroys bacteria (12)

DOWN

2 Cattle thief (7)
3 Rent (4)
4 Private soldier in the Royal Engineers (6)
5 Studying just before an exam (8)
6 Carried (something heavy) (5)
7 Ruin (12)
8 Metamorphosed (12)
13 Grizzle (8)
16 Indisputable (7)
17 Audible and uncontrolled expulsion of air through nose and mouth (6)
19 Wastes time (5)
21 Fissure in something (4)

Solution see page 288

222

ACROSS

1 Old banger (6)
4 Undies (6)
8 Spanish bites? (5)
9 Dewilder (7)
10 State represented by Senators Barry Goldwater and John McCain (7)
11 Useful possession (5)
12 Temporary access to a docked vessel (9)
17 Close-fitting (5)
19 Venetian taxi? (7)
21 Heads (of a coin) (7)
22 Voucher (5)
23 Rinse the throat (6)
24 Semi–liquid mixture of water and cement or manure, say (6)

DOWN

1 Body's disruption after a long flight (3,3)
2 Large plover (7)
3 Green sauce (5)
5 North–western state bordering Canada (7)
6 Name of eighteen undisputed kings of France (5)
7 Perspiring (6)
9 Fizz (9)
13 Innate — unprocessed (7)
14 It bangs on a door (7)
15 Potent (6)
16 Cheerful (6)
18 Donor (5)
20 About birth (5)

Solution see page 288

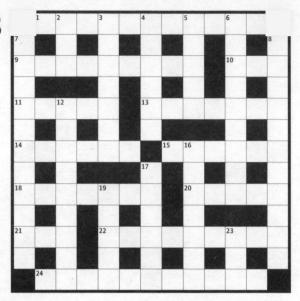

ACROSS

1 Essential bit of badminton equipment (11)

9 Second in command (6,3)

10 Whopper (3)

11 Punch (5)

13 What Oscar Wilde called 'the unspeakable in full pursuit of the uneatable' (3,4)

14 Vehicle drawn by a bullock (6)

15 Something with an elongated rectangular shape (6)

18 Move about ponderously (7)

20 Former US World No 1 tennis player, b. 1954 (5)

21 Time (3)

22 Legion (9)

24 Attractive (3-8)

DOWN

2 Sing with the mouth shut (3)

3 One undertaking an arduous journey in difficult country (7)

4 Allow to escape punishment (3,3)

5 Kind of pastry used for eclairs (5)

6 Substance in plants — so cull eel (anag) (9)

7 Skier's eye protection (4,7)

8 Assemble (3,8)

12 Providing necessary support (9)

16 Imperfection (7)

17 Swiss-style holiday house (6)

19 Imitate in order to ridicule (5)

23 Large pot for making tea (3)

Solution see page 288

224

ACROSS

1 Minor transgression (10)

7 Set of computer icons, clicked on for functions (7)

8 Sacred poem (written by King David?) (5)

10 Prod (4)

11 Glancing blow (8)

13 Nuance (6)

15 Out-of-control child (6)

17 Stranger (8)

18 Unsightly (4)

21 Exclusive news story (5)

22 Chaos (7)

23 Indecent behaviour (10)

DOWN

1 Cheap red or white (5)

2 Raise to the third power (4)

3 Filled with concern (6)

4 Unsuitable (8)

5 Tanned hide (7)

6 Phenomenal (10)

9 Petrol-driven two-wheeler (10)

12 Largest country of the Horn of Africa (8)

14 Conductor by which electricity leaves a device (7)

16 Frenetic (6)

19 Radiant beauty (5)

20 Accurate (4)

Solution see page 288

SOLUTIONS

1

```
P U R I S T   A M O U N T
O   O   T     A   N     O
L I M B O   W A D D I N G
I   A   N   I   E   F   G
C O N D E M N   I D Y L L
Y   C     D   R       E
  E V A P O R A T E
A     R   W     X   B
B A S I S   B U T C H E R
S   P   E   O   O     E
E Q U I N O X   T A B L E
N   R   A     A   I   Z
T A N G L E   B L I T H E
```

2

```
  A S Y L U M S E E K E R
T   E   E   E V   R   E
H E A T S   A T A L O S S
U   S   T   S   N     O
N A I L   B L U E B E L L
D   D   W   Y   S     U
E V E N I F   O C E L O T
R   N   U   E   O   E
F I E L D I N G   R U I N
L   X   F   L   A   R   E
A T P E A C E   K U D O S
S   E   L   S   I   E   S
H E L P L E S S N E S S
```

3

```
W O M B A T   T U T T U T
E   I   R   B   N   R   H
A R T I C L E   C A I R O
L   R   A   Y   U   U   R
T W E E D   O T T O M A N
H   I     N     P   Y
  D A Y A N D N I G H T
S   L   D   R     R
P A L E R M O   I S S U E
R   E   I   U   D   I   A
U R G E S   B L I N D E R
C   E   E   T   U   E   E
E N D I N G   A M U S E D
```

4

```
    P   P   B   S
    I R R I T A B L E
  P   O   S   C   A   F
P U M P   C L A Y M O R E
  R   E   E   L     A
S C O R E S   L A M E N T
  H   T     I   K
C A N Y O N   B E L O N G
  S   A   O   L   E
H E A T H R O W   I F S O
  R   O N   M   B   S
  P O L I C E M A N
  L   A   N   R
```

SOLUTIONS

5

```
 CRYSTALBALL
KIT  T  A  Y G
IMPERIOUS  TAU
N   U  N I T T
GRIND CONCEIT
D  N E E  L E
OCCULT PEWTER
M  I  C N O P
CADAVER INNER
O E I  U G  E
MEN OPTIMISTS
E C L C A E S
 METAPHYSICS
```

6

```
 BRACEANDBIT
L U O F E  N T
INTERPRET AXE
N  S  I E B E
GAMMA CURTAIN
U I G  A  D Y
INLIEU COBWEB
S K  W F A  O
TITULAR FRYUP
I O E  E I  P
COO ARTICHOKE
S T S C E U R
 THATCHERITE
```

7

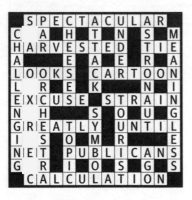

```
 SPECTACULAR
C A H T N S  M
HARVESTED TIE
A  E A  R A
LOOKS CARTOON
L R E K  N I
EXCUSE STRAIN
N H  S O U G
GREATLY UNTIL
I S O M R  E
NET PUBLICANS
G R I O S G S
 CALCULATION
```

8

```
CONTEMPLATIVE
R A E I  R  O
EDEN ANNUALLY
I G N E I  E
ANYOLDIRON
A E  E   I
BRACER CARAFE
Y O  A  N
 OPENLETTER
C L T Y I E
LAMBCHOP TIDY
V A E S A B
GEIGERCOUNTER
```

```
C O L D H E A R T E D L Y
O   E E   W   A   I   E
P E C K I S H   K I N G S
    T   R   I   E   E   T
C R U X   A L A C A R T E
A   R   S   E   A     R
P I E R C E   E R O D E D
I   H   D   E   E     A
N A R C O T I C   S T A Y
H   O   O   C   D   R
A L L I N   T E A C A K E
N   L   E   U   W   C   N
D I S C R I M I N A T E D
```

```
      S O U L M U S I C
S   H E   P   O   T   O
T W I N E   D E C L A I M
O   P   D   A   K   I   M
C A P A C I T Y   U N D O
K   O   O   E   M   E   N
I M P U R E   W I N D O W
N   O   N   S   S   G   E
T O T E   M A N T I L L A
R   A   A   F   R   A   L
A M M O N I A   I N S E T
D   U   O   R   A   S   H
E S S E N T I A L
```

```
      O N T H E W I N G
B   M   V   I X   N   O
E L A T E   T I P S T E R
V   R   R   I   O   E   D
E U R O S T A R   B R I O
R   I   E   N   B   M   N
L E A K E R   C A R E E R
Y   G   N   S   R   D   A
H E E D   A P H O R I S M
I   A   C   O   N   A   S
L A B C O A T   E X T R A
L   L   O   O   S   E   Y
S E E D L I N G S
```

```
B A T T L E   C A T T L E
E   O   U   B   H   N
R O M A N   W O R K I N G
A   M   G   I   E   E   U
T A I L E N D   A W F U L
E   E   E   S       F
      S A R C A S T I C
C   E   N     O   S
O A S T S   G I V E N U P
S   W   T   L   I   K   A
S K I F F L E   S C O U R
E   F   U   T   U   S
T A T T L E   R A T T L E
```

SOLUTIONS

13

SUPPLICATE / JOAOUH / ALLEGRO LARCH / CAEKDIA / KIRK MOREOVER / TRNSED / HUGGED HANSEL / EIITCY / LAVENDER ABLE / AESDCAV / DOWSE INHASTE / ARUAIR / SYSTEMATIC

14

15

16

17

```
.PREPOSITION.
M I O   T E   B   E
EAGERNESS   SAX
N     T A   T   T A
DONNE   DASHING
E   I N   Y     N G
LOCATE   ESCAPE
S   A     S T   T R
SERVANT   OMEGA
O   A   D A M   A
HUG   MARMALADE
N U   I   V C M D
.BATTLESHIPS.
```

18

```
BENIGNNEGLECT
A A   O O   A C R
TETANUS   MELBA
  U   E H   B A P
SORT   FULLSTOP
N A   C   P I   I
OILCAN   UNDIES
W   R   A G   N T
DEPUTISE   ACES
O O   L   S A   H
NAIRA   UPSWING
I S   N   M I N A
ABERDEENANGUS
```

19

```
  LOCALDERBY
O A U   A P U
BUGBEAR   INFER
S E S   R S F I
ECRU   AUTOBAHN
Q   I   P D L G
URSINE   RIPOFF
I I S   W C   I
OUTSTRIP   YAWN
U D A   S Z U G
SWORN   DWINDLE
  W C   O Z I R
  INTERMEZZO
```

20

```
  CONSUMMATE
  R E S   I   R G
SEAMLESS   AWRY
  E E   R T I U
  PUSH   PRELUDE
    I   C E     G
  MISCONSTRUE
  U   N   S A
TESTIFY   ADDS
  S A E   N I P
BLAB   TWOFACED
  I O T   N N L
  HORIZONTAL
```

SOLUTIONS

21

22

23

24

25

```
R O B U S T A C O F F E E
E L   L   R   N   R     S
L E A   A T A N Y C O S T
I   C   P   B   X   M   U
C A K E H O L E   S T O A
    P   E   E   B   H   R
F L O R A L   L O V E L Y
U   O   D   K   N   W
C O L A   C U B E R O O T
H   R   E   W   I   R   H
S N O W B O A R D   D U O
I   C   R   I   L   G   R
A S K F O R T H E M O O N
```

26

```
      S U B N O R M A L
H   G   C   U   N   E   A
O P R A H   R H U B A R B
U   A   E   S   S   N   O
S U P E R M A N   E S A U
E   H   Z   R   D   P   R
S P I G O T   F I L I A L
P   C   S   W   V   R   E
A N N E   J A P O N I C A
R   O   M   S   R   T   D
R I V I E R A   C R E T E
O   E   R   B   E   D   R
W O L V E R I N E
```

27

```
  M I N D B O G G L I N G
S   N   U   U   O   B   E
M O T I F   T R A N S I T
A   R   F   S   T   E   R
A S H U N   H E L S I N K I
H   D   S   T   K       C
A L E P P O   K I R S C H
N       E   C   N   P   Q
D E M O C R A T   G U R U
G   A   I   R   S   T   I
R E P R O V E   T U N I C
A   L   U   S   A   I   K
B R E A S T S T R O K E
```

28

```
C A R D I A C   I   A   B
O   E   C   A D M I R E R
S I T W E L L   P   M   I
T   R   C   L E E W A R D
S C O U R   U   R   D   G
    O   E X P A T I A T E
    O   A       U       A
A L T I M E T E R       K
U   R   S   I   B A G E L
B O U D O I R   A   A   O
U   S   D   A L B U M E N
R U T L A N D   L   U   E
N   Y   S   E L E C T O R
```

29

```
C A L L E D T O M I N D
S Q   A   O   P   N   I
T R U S S   R E P R E S S
U A   T   S O   R   C
P A T E   F A L S E T T O
E   I   P   L   I   N
F I C K L E   S N A C K S
A     E   M   G   H   O
C E R E B R U M   W A I L
T   E   E   S   W   U   A
I T A L I C S   A S C O T
O   L   A   E   R   E   E
N O M E N C L A T U R E
```

30

```
          L I F E C Y C L E
B   L   I   E   A   L   L
O C E A N   C O N C E D E
U   X   O   U   T   V   C
Q U I S L I N G   P E A T
U   C   E D   S   R   R
E X O D U S   N U N C I O
T   G   M   E   N   L   P
G O R Y   E G G S H E L L
A   A   E   G   H   V   A
R O P E D I N   A G E N T
N   H   G   O   D   R   E
I V Y L E A G U E
```

31

```
  T O W E R B L O C K
  H   A   A   I   A   C
G I N S L I N G   B A R B
E   T   L   H   A   E
F A R E   S T I L T E D
    E   W   E       P
  C A L L I G R A P H Y
  R   S   S   L
F A T C A T S   G A W P
  D   I   E   G   C   I
S L U R   R E L I A B L E
  E   C   I   U   T   O
  M A N A G E M E N T
```

32

```
  L I F E G U A R D S
  A   A   R   R   A   P
S T O R T I N G   N O O K
E   R   P   U   C   R
R U I N   A M N E S T Y
    E   B   E       A
  C U R T A I N C A L L
  H   C   T   L
B E S P O K E   G L A D
R   A   C   C   O   E
B R A T   H E A T W A V E
Y   I   A   T   E   O
  S O U T H S U D A N
```

33

```
    A C O U S T I C S
W S N   U E   N   L
H O I S T   S I R O C C O
A X   E   T F O   A
T W O F A C E D   I N O N
S   F   T D G S   E
C U T L E T   L A B O U R
O   H R   C V   L   A
O P E L   A U T O B A H N
K B D   C   T B G
I C E R I N K   T U L L E
N S S   O E   E R
G E T A C R O S S
```

34

```
C A N T A T A   C S   S
R A T   S C R A T C H
E G O T R I P   O A   O
E M I   E N S U R E D
D Y I N G   C S C   D
  A   H I T T H E H A Y
  R T   A   S
O D D M A N O U T   I
I I N V   C U F F S
L A S A G N E   H E Y
M T L   R A I N I E R
A N I S E E D   N G I
N L S   O R G A N Z A
```

35

```
R E C E D E   W A R M U P
E A R D P C L
B A R N O N E   P I Q U E
U E P S A U A
F O R G O   T E L L E R S
F U I E E
  C O N T E N T M E N T
S I A O A
C U L V E R T   U P S E T
E S L I N U O
N A K E D   O C T A G O N
T I E N E A E
S U N D R Y   A D O R E D
```

36

```
G A M E P L A N   S L A V
A E U N S I I
S I M O N   G E T E V E N
H E C E A E T
  I N T H E L O N G R U N
A T A S D E
C R O W N S   T I N D E R
O D U N R S
L A D Y J A N E G R E Y
Y R U W F S H
T W A D D L E   I N D I A
E W Y L R E L
S O N G   F L A M I N G O
```

SOLUTIONS

37

```
F U M B L E . S P A R K S
U Y . E . R . O . . A
L H A S A . T O O M U C H
M N . P . U . W . T . A
A M M E T E R . L O S E R . A
R . A . N . E . . A
. R E M A I N D E R .
P . I . N . A . C
P I N C U R . G E N U I N E
L U . R . I . O . S . R
F O R L O R N . R A I S E
E B . R . . S . N . A
R E S I S T . W E A S E L
```

38

```
. P R A I S E . P I O U S
. R . R . E . A . P . A
L O I T E R . S N A T C H
. W . D . E . I . I . A
P E T E . N E W C O M E R
. S . C . G . H . A . A
S T O N E C I R C L E .
R . O . . T . M . A . S
A Q U A R I U S . L O P E
S . G . E . I . O . O
C O H E R E . C I R R U S
A . E . U . . A . I . S
L E N I N . S L E E V E
```

39

```
. P A C K I N G C A S E .
S W . N . U . A . E . C
C O N C O R D A T . M A O
R . C . I . E . I . N
A L A C K . S T R I F E S
T . L . O . M . I . T
C E M E N T . B R U N E I
H . A . S . I . A . P
C O M M E N T . V O L G A
A . A . R . Y . I . T
R U T . N U M B E R O N E
D . E . S . I . R . V . D
. F R I T T E R A W A Y .
```

40

```
T O P U T I T M I L D L Y
O . Y . H . Y . G . E . E
W A R . E U P H O R B I A
E . A . S . I . R . T . R
L A M P P O S T . M O O N
. I . I . T . M . R . E
B E D L A M . K A I S E R
A . S . N . H . N . P
Y U C K . C O R P O R A L
L . H . T . T . O . I . A
E Y E S H A D O W . S O N
A . M . A . O . E . O . K
F E E D I N G F R E N Z Y
```

41

```
CAME CHILDISH
O O T O I M U
NEWDEAL FEMUR
F E E E T E T
LURCH INSANE
I R E N S E
CONFECTIONERY
T O H N E
 ONESIE TRIES
E P C W O D I
POLAR AMUSING
E U U L R O H
ENSEMBLE EMIT
```

42

```
SOFT JOYSTICK
C A D A B A
OUCH ADULTERY
R E P I A X O
SOCKITTOME
E A C Y A S D
STRIKE UNIQUE
E D A L D U L
 INVETERATE
A B D N R D G
GOURMAND ARIA
A L I O O T
RELAXING ONCE
```

43

```
CONSIDERATION
O E N I D N O
AIL CATHARSIS
S S E H M I W
TROUNCED AGUE
 N S R S N A
PUMMEL SPOILT
A A D M H F
LAND TITANIUM
A D S C G C O
CRESTARUN ADO
E L A O U N C
SLANGINGMATCH
```

44

```
 QUADRANGLE
HU I A E E
ABANDON UTTER
R L E D R D E
DUMB SONOROUS
B R M T W T
ORGIES SINNER
I E L R C A
LISTENED TAXI
E T V G T R N
DRAMA AGONISE
 P N I T E D
 COTTONWOOL
```

SOLUTIONS

45

```
R O B U S T ▪ N I M B U S
A   A   C   P   M O   L
D E S P A I R ▪ P E N N E
I   T   L   O   L   A   U
S T E E P ▪ B A Y O N E T
H   E   A   ▪   Z   H
▪ U T I L I T A R I A N ▪
C   O   I   A       P
O N T H E G O ▪ M E D I A
S   A   S   N   B   E   P
M U L E S ▪ E C L I P S E
O   L   E   R   E   O   R
S A Y I N G ▪ G R A T I S
```

46

```
S I M P L E ▪ E S C H E W
T   A   I       U O   A
U T U R N ▪ L A M P R E Y
B   N   G   I   M   D   L
B E D R O C K ▪ O M E G A
Y   E   E   N       S   Y
▪ R E H E A R S A L ▪
F   E   S       O   I
E M B E R ▪ H A N D B A G
N   O   O   O   U   S   N
D I A R I S T ▪ D I T T O
E   S   N   G   E   R
R A T H E R ▪ D E G R E E
```

47

```
H A I R S P L I T T I N G
L   E   A   G   I   A
F L A B ▪ R E L A T I V E
I   E   A   O   T   Y
A N G L O P H O N E ▪
A   A   E   R   S
E L I C I T ▪ M A S T I C
L   O   I       N
▪ U N A S S U M I N G ▪
P   R   R   L   A   F
M A N I T O B A ▪ N E E D
L   E   M   I   N   I
F L O R A A N D F A U N A
```

48

```
H U M P B A C K ▪ H A I R
A   O   O   A   F   D   O
I N C U R ▪ T R E L L I S
L   K   E   C   V   I   E
▪ B E N D T H E E L B O W
C   R   T   Y   R       O
L A Y L O W ▪ F I A S C O
U   T   M   S   I   D
B I B L E B A S H I N G ▪
L   A   I   N   C   C
A D M I R A L ▪ E L E G Y
N   B   S   E   S   R   S
D R I P ▪ P R O S P E C T
```

49

```
M O R R I S D A N C I N G
  R   O   C L   L   U
Z I N G   U B I Q U I T Y
  G   U   F   V   T   S
S I D E E F F E C T
  N   L       E   M
M A T U R E   U P R O A R
  L   P   T       T
    F O X T E R R I E R
  B   R   H   N   O   R
T I M O R O U S   M A I D
  R   N   S   I   E   E
F O O T B A L L P O O L S
```

50

```
R O C K E T S C I E N C E
O   A   P   O   R   Y   X
B U S T I E R   O X L I P
    C   C   B   Q   O   L
Z E A L   S E Q U E N C E
E   D   A   T   O     T
I B E R I A   B I K I N I
T     R   T   S   C   V
G A M E B I R D   C E D E
E   O   O   I   C   C
I D L E R   V U L T U R E
S   A   N   I   U   B   F
T H R E E D A Y E V E N T
```

51

```
S O T T O V O C E   J   M
  V   U   I   A   F E T A
H U R R I C A N E   L   N
  M   K   T   N   F L O G
I   O   F O Y E R   Y   A
C O F F E R   D U R B A N
E   F   D     G   E   E
H O T T U B   U B O A T S
O   H   P O T T Y   N   E
C H E W   W   O K   S
K   P   S L I P K N O T S
E V E N   E   I   O   U
Y   G   B R O A D B A N D
```

52

```
      P   B   F   D
  B E A R   I L L W I L L
  Y   L   G   E   S   A
B E A M   O V E R T O P S
  X       T   T   R   O
A T H E A R T   B E E F Y
  E   X   Y   F   S   H
S N A P S   M A N S I O N
  S   O   B   L       N
B I E N N I A L   M O O N
  O   E   D   O   U   U
N O N S E Q U I T U R
      T   T   T   E
```

SOLUTIONS

53

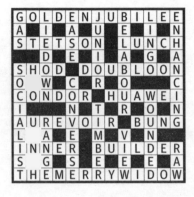

54

55

56

57

```
. H U S B A N D I N G .
A . O . E . I . E . I .
T U R F W A R . F U N G I
T . U . N . I . E . . N .
H U S K . B E N N E V I S
E . . . D . R . D . E . U
R E M A I N . Z E P H Y R
E . A . S . T . R . . . G
A M R I T S A R . F R E E
D . M . I . H . C . E . N
Y E A R N . I D Y L L I C
. R . C . T . A . A . . Y
W A L T D I S N E Y . . .
```

58

```
E X M O O R . S C R I P T
F . A . V . H . N . . R .
F O R T E . B R A V E R Y
I . Q . R . A . P . P . I
G L U T T O N . L E T O N G
Y . E . . . Q . E . . . G
. E N C O U N T E R . . .
H . . O . E . . A . . P .
A D M I N . T H U N D E R
N . U . S . T . N . I . .
S U C R O S E . D E A L S
O . U . L . . U . N . . O
M A S S E S . N E W T O N
```

59

```
M U T U A L . T R A G I C
I . U . L . . E . R . . O
D O G M A . R E A D I L Y
O . B . R . I . L . M . O
F R O G M A N . I N E P T
F . A . G . S . . . . . E
. T E S T A M E N T . . .
S . . Q . B . . R . F . .
H A I K U . E V A C U E E
U . N . E . L . R . F . R
C O N C E A L . G O F E R
K . E . Z . . O . L . . E
S E R V E R . I N S E C T
```

60

```
I N M Y B O O K . C L E F
N . U . I . C . G . A . I
F U S E D . C L O S U R E
O . I . E . U . W . G . N
. A C C O M P L I S H E D
S . A . N . Y . T . . . I
T A L K E D . T H A M E S
R . S . U . A . O . . . H
A S O F T E N A S N O T .
N . I . I . F . W . R . B
D I L E M M A . I N A N E
E . E . E . I . N . G . N
D I R E . F R A G M E N T
```

SOLUTIONS

61

62

63

64

65

```
D R E S S E D T O K I L L
I N   K   E   U   R   I
T A G   I N T E R L O C K
C L   P   E   S   N   A
H A I R L E S S   L I M B
  S   A   T   D   N   L
S P H I N X   T I N G L E
H   S   E   P   S   B
A P E X   S O F T S O A P
L   T   K   T   A   A   O
L U T H E R A N S   R A W
O   E   L   T   T   D   E
W O R D P R O C E S S O R
```

66

```
      V   T   F   S
  T H E R A P E U T I C
  U   E   C   M   A   A
S T I R   T I M E L E S S
  T       I   E   W   E
M I S S I L E   C A C H E
  F   K   E   L   R   I
F R A I L   F A N T A S Y
  U   R   F   W       T
S T I M U L U S   C R O W
  T   I   O   U   O   R
  I N S T A B I L I T Y
    H   T   T   L
```

67

```
S T O C K E X C H A N G E
  E   R   X   I   N   L
M E M O   H Y D R O G E N
  T   O   I   E   M   E
K O O K A B U R R A
  T   I       L   M
P A R R O T   H E Y D A Y
  L   O   A       J
    W E B B R O W S E R
  H   L   L   D   A   S
D E M O L I S H   V O T E
  R   C   N   A   E   I
F O R K L I F T T R U C K
```

68

```
  C O N T R I V A N C E
P   W   A   N   B   A   I
H U E A N D C R Y   R A N
I   G   O   S   D   D
L A P E L   M A S S I V E
O   A   E   E       N   P
S T R I D E   M I D D L E
O   T       E   N   E   N
P E R P L E X   F I X E D
H   I   A   E   E       E
E N D   S A M A R I T A N
R   G   T   P   N   E   T
  S E N S A T I O N A L
```

SOLUTIONS

69

70

71

72

73

```
. B R A N D T . . C O M B O
O . U . E . . . H . U . U .
M O R S E L . T E A S E S .
. K . T . I . . S . T . T .
S I R E . R A G T R A D E .
. S . R . I . Y . . N . D .
. H A E M O R R H A G E . .
B . P . . U . O . . P . A .
E M P H A S I S . O G R E .
A . E . L . . C . S . W . .
R E A L L Y . O U T F O X .
U . S . O . . P . . L . R .
P I E T Y . R E D E E M . .
```

74

```
. S Y C O P H A N T S .
. H . O . A . D . I . G
C A V A L I E R . G R O G
. G . S . R . I . O . B
. S A T E . W A N N A B E
. . A . T . T . . L .
W O L F W H I S T L E .
O . . . E . C . . O .
A B D O M E N . Q U I Z
B . P . Z . V . G . O
B L U E . E P I P H A N Y
E . R . R . E . . I . A
. D A I S Y W H E E L .
```

75

```
I N C O N S I D E R A T E
. A . U . T . U . E . A .
R U S T . A B N E G A T E
. S . D . N . C . A . A .
S E C O N D B E S T . . .
. A . . . B . . . T . F .
S T U R D Y . O R A T O R
E . H . . . B . . . R .
. . U N A S S I S T E D .
. T . B . L . E . C . B .
R E T A I L E R . R E E L
. L . R . A . V . E . A .
O L D B O Y N E T W O R K
```

76

```
A N T I C L I M A C T I C
V . H . L . N . L . O . H
O R E . I N S O L E N C E
I . F . Q . E . Y . G . A
D A I Q U I R I . G U S T
. . R . I . T . C . E . O
F L I M S Y . R A I S I N
E . N . H . S . R . W .
T O G S . I M M O L A T E
L . L . L . O . U . G . A
O V I P A R O U S . G U T
C . N . O . C . E . E . I
K E E P S T H E L I D O N
```

SOLUTIONS

77

E	X	H	I	B	I	T	I	O	N	I	S	M
R		I		I		I		A		N		I
G	A	G		P	O	L	I	T	I	C	A	L
O		H		L		L		S		O		I
T	E	E	N	A	G	E	R		O	M	I	T
		X		N		R		R		M		I
D	A	P	P	E	R		M	E	D	U	S	A
E		L		S		S		V		N		
M	O	O	D		A	P	P	E	T	I	T	E
O		S		A		L		I		C		X
T	R	I	E	N	N	I	A	L		A	C	T
E		V		T		N		L		D		O
D	Y	E	D	I	N	T	H	E	W	O	O	L

78

D	E	C	O	N	T	A	M	I	N	A	T	E
U		A		O		C		L		U		V
O	U	T	P	O	S	T		L	A	D	L	E
		E		K		I		F		I		R
P	A	R	T		F	O	R	A	S	O	N	G
O		E		R		N		T				R
T	U	R	E	E	N		F	E	E	B	L	E
E			D		C		D		L		E	
N	O	T	I	O	N	A	L		T	U	R	N
T		W		L		L		S		B		
A	L	I	K	E		I	N	H	A	B	I	T
T		N		N		C		O		E		A
E	L	E	C	T	I	O	N	E	E	R	E	D

79

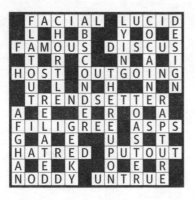

	F	A	C	I	A	L		L	U	C	I	D
	L		H		B			Y		O		E
F	A	M	O	U	S		D	I	S	C	U	S
	T		R		C		N		A			I
H	O	S	T		O	U	T	G	O	I	N	G
	U		L		N		H		N			N
	T	R	E	N	D	S	E	T	T	E	R	
A		E		E		R		O		A		
F	I	L	I	G	R	E	E		A	S	P	S
G		A		E		U		S		T		
H	A	T	R	E	D		P	U	T	O	U	T
A		E		K		O		E		R		
N	O	D	D	Y		U	N	T	R	U	E	

80

T	H	R	E	E	P	E	N	N	Y	B	I	T
A		E		N		N		O		R		E
R	E	M	O	V	E	D		B	A	I	R	N
		A		Y		U		I		E		A
C	H	I	N		P	R	O	L	I	F	I	C
H		N		I		E		I				I
A	S	S	U	M	E		S	T	U	C	C	O
I			M		D		Y		H		U	
N	E	G	L	I	G	E	E		P	A	S	S
M		R		N		L		S		N		
A	B	I	D	E		P	A	N	A	C	E	A
I		E		N		H		A		E		I
L	I	G	H	T	F	I	N	G	E	R	E	D

81

```
P A P A C Y   D O D G E
R   I   A     O   E   N
D U L C E T   S U B S E T
  D   A   E     B   E   I
F E E S   R H E T O R I C
  N   S   W   T   T   E
  T R O J A N H O R S E
D   I   U   I     E   R
V I N D A L O O   B L U B
O   G   G   P   E   D
R O L L O N   I S C H I A
A   E   N     A   C   T
K I T T Y   U N S A F E
```

82

```
S A L V A T I O N A R M Y
U   O   I   W   L   I
O V I D   M O N U M E N T
  E   K   B   E   O   T
A R M A G E D D O N   I
  G   R       D   I
S N A K E S   C O S I N E
  E   I       H   T
    L I O N E L B A R T
M   L   S   C   R   U
B A S I L I S K   E D D Y
  G   N   E   U   A   E
J I G G E R Y P O K E R Y
```

83

```
F A L S E E C O N O M Y
C D   T   S   P   P   E
H E A D Y   C A P I T A L
R   P   X   O   O   I   L
I O T A   P R O S E C C O
S   O   S   T   I       W
T O R P O R   S T E N C H
C   M   B   E   E   A
H I G H B R O W   D R U M
U   E   R   T   W   V   M
R E T R E A T   O Z O N E
C   O   R   L   L   U   R
H A N D O V E R F I S T
```

84

```
      C   W   U   F
W O O D E N S P O O N
O   M   D   U   U   O
D R A B   L E A R N I N G
D       O   L   D   S
O F F S I C K   W O O E D
O   L   K   M   U   N
G R O A T   M A L T E S E
W   P   D   R       I
H O O D W I N K   B U C K
R   A   V   E   U   A
D I S T A S T E F U L
    H   N   S   F
```

SOLUTIONS

85

86

87

88

89

```
E L E P H A N T S H R E W
A   X   Y   O   P   O   H
T I C   P R O S E L Y T E
E   L   N   K   Y   A   E
N E U R O S I S   C L O D
    S   T   E   P   A   L
A S I T I S   S L U I C E
E   O   C   B   A   R
R E N D   B E A T I F I C
O   Z   F   A   Y   O   A
S H O W I N G U P   R I B
O   N   S   L   U   C   I
L I E C H T E N S T E I N
```

90

```
A B H O R R E D   C A L M
L   U   E   X   M   B   O
T A M I L   C R O W B A R
O   D   I   E   U   O   I
  F R A N K S I N A T R A
C   U   Q   S   T   R
O S M I U M   C A C H E T
N       I   S   I   O   Y
C H A I S E L O N G U E
L   L   H   I   L   D   E
A N T W E R P   I L I A D
V   E   D   U   N   G
E A R S   O P E N F I R E
```

91

```
M A I D S O F H O N O U R
  S   O   B   A   U   G
U S E S   S I L E N T L Y
  A   E   E   V   N   Y
W I N D E R M E R E
  L   V   R   C
N E S S I E   B A Y E R N
  D   P   L   O
    L E P R E C H A U N
  M   I   L   M   U   P
P A S T R A M I   M A I N
  Z   U   I   S   I   E
L E A P I N T H E D A R K
```

92

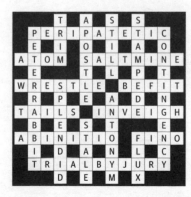

```
    T   A   S   S
P E R I P A T E T I C
E   I   O   I   A   O
A T O M   S A L T M I N E
E   T   L   P   T
W R E S T L E   B E F I T
R   P   E   A   D   N
T A I L S   I N V E I G H
B   E   S   T   E
A B I N I T I O   F I N O
I   D   A   N   L   C
  T R I A L B Y J U R Y
  D   E   M   X
```

SOLUTIONS

97

```
D E C K   D A N B R O W N
O H     N   R   U   O
L O I N   U N B I A S E D
D   P   G   U   D   T   E
R E M A R K A B L E
U   U   A   L   E   L   C
M I N U T E   A P P E A R
S   K   U   B   A   M   E
      D I S A S T R O U S
F   R   T   T   H   N   C
L O O K I N T O   W A D E
A   P   E   E       D   N
T R E A S U R E   W E P T
```

98

```
M A S K   T E E N A G E R
I   Q     I   E   A   E
S L U R   E G G W H I T E
S   A   H   H   S   T   F
T I N S E L T O W N
A   D   A   H   O   D   B
T R E N D Y   A R D O U R
E   R   H   S   T   G   A
        J U M P T H E G U N
O   T   N   R   Y   E   D
K H A R T O U M   W R E N
R   C   E   C       E   E
A R T E R I E S   S L O W
```

99

```
  P A C K E D   P I P E R
  E   H   A   R   U   E
B A Z A A R   W A L R U S
  C   T   M   D   V   U
C O D E   A Q U A R I U M
  C   A   R   N   E   E
  K N U C K L E D O W N
U   E   E   A   R   U
S Q U A N D E R   E A R L
E   T   E   T   G   T
F O R C E D   H I A T U S
U   A   D   L   N   R
L O L L Y   B Y G O N E
```

100

```
N A M E   M A N D I B L E
E   A     M   E   I   E
A I R Y   B A S E B A L L
R   I   V   Z   P   S   S
M O N T E N E G R O
I   E   R   D   O   E   G
S H R I M P   D O W N E R
S   S   I   H   T   T   E
      O C T A H E D R O N
M   S   E   T   D   E   A
I M P O L I T E   M A R C
N   U   L   E       T   H
D E R R I E R E   T Y K E
```

SOLUTIONS

101

102

103

104

105

```
B U G S _ T W O F A C E D
Y . U . P . I . R . Y . R
D E S C E N D . O N C U E
E . T . G . E . S . L . Y
S C O W L . O X T A I L .
I . . . E . F . . . N . A
G O I N G S T R A I G H T
N . M . H . B . . . T . .
_ A P A C H E . R O M E O
B . R . O . M . O . O . R
A M O U R . A L A D D I N
C . V . P . R . D . E . E
K E E P S A K E _ C L A Y
```

106

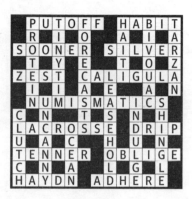

```
P U T O F F _ H A B I T
R . I . O . A . I . A
S O O N E R _ S I L V E R
T . Y . E . T . O . Z
Z E S T _ C A L I G U L A
I . I . A . E . A . N
N U M I S M A T I C S
C . N . T . S . N . H
L A C R O S S E _ D R I P
U . A . C . H . U . N
T E N N E R _ O B L I G E
C . N . A . L . G . L
H A Y D N _ A D H E R E
```

107

```
P A R A D E _ H E A D E D
U . E . S . X . O . I
P L A T E A U _ T I L E S
I . C . P . B . R . P . A
L I T H E _ T E A C H E R
S . . . S . R . . . I . M
_ C O N T R A S T I N G
S . U . C . R . . . J
P A T I E N T _ A L O N E
R . C . I . I . F . C . R
A M O N G _ O F F I C E S
N . M . H . N . I . U . E
G U E S T S _ S C U R V Y
```

108

```
. . . L O B P .
. I F Y O U P L E A S E
. M . O . T . E . S . X
S P I N _ T R A N S E P T
E . . . A . T . O . E
T R O T S K Y _ E V E N T
I . E . E . H . E . D
F A U L T _ G E O R D I E
L . E . K . A . . . T
L I S T E N E R _ C R U X
S . E . A . I . H . R
M E X I C A N W A V E
. T . K . G . D
```

SOLUTIONS

109

110

111

112

113

```
M U G A B E     M I L E S
  A   R   Y   I   E   T
S C R A P S   A N T H E R
  A   P   T   O   A   I
A D E N   A P P R O V E D
  A   E   N   L   R   E
  M A L A D J U S T E D
A   F   E   N   R   I
D E F E R R E D   E D G Y
U   I   A   E   A   R
L A X I T Y   R E D E E M
T   E   T   E   L   S
S A D L Y   A D D E R S
```

114

```
L E A T H E R J A C K E T
O   N   O   O   F   N   H
W I T   N U M B E R O N E
E   I   O   A   W   C   R
R A C K R E N T   S K Y E
    O   A   Y   T   O   A
M E A G R E   C O R N E T
I   G   Y   H   X   E
L O U T   P A R A F F I N
K   L   S   R   E   F   I
S T A T E R O O M   E Y E
O   N   T   L   I   C   C
P I T C H E D B A T T L E
```

115

```
L A I R   F A C T O T U M
A   N       M   H   A   A
N I C K   P A R R O T E D
D   R   A   Z   E   E   E
F R E E B O O T E R
I   A   E   N   S   Z   U
L O S E R S   A C T I O N
L   E   R   F   O   M   T
    F A V O U R A B L E
S   N   T   S   E   A   N
H Y A C I N T H   I B I D
O   S   O   E       W   E
T R A I N E R S   F E U D
```

116

```
      P   E   S   Z
  C R O W N J E W E L S
  L   K   A   A   R   E
W A R Y   C O M M O N L Y
Y     T   Y   H   F
S P A M M E R   W O T A N
I   E   D   A   U   S
A G G R O   A C T R E S S
E   I   B   R       U
C O R D U R O Y   F U R Y
N   I   I   L   A   E
S M A L L M I N D E D
  N   L   C   E
```

SOLUTIONS

117

```
P I C K L E   S A U C E S
O   A   E   C   L   A   H
M A R C O N I   A T R I A
A   O   T   R   M   I   G
D E L T A   C O O L B A G
E   R   U   O   Y
  P A N D E M O N I U M
A   C   S   I       W
S T I C K U P   G A F F E
H   D   N   E   H   R   A
R A I T A   C A T W A L K
A   T   V   T   I   M   E
M A Y H E M   D E M E A N
```

118

```
J U N I P E R   Q   G   M
A   I   E   A C U T E L Y
M E G A T O N   A   M   R
E   E   R   D E N T I S T
S A L V O   O   T   N   L
  L   L I M O U S I N E
  D   S   M   O
L I G H T S O U T   G
I   E   A   L   H A V O C
C H E A T E D   E   I   H
H   Z   I   I R O N O R E
E Y E S O R E   R   L   C
N   R   N   S K Y L A R K
```

119

```
T U C K   S A L A R I E D
A   E   P   R   D   U
I O N A   N A U T I L U S
L   O   F   T   N   E   T
B U T T O N H O O K
A   A   U   Y   U   S   G
C O P E R S   A V O W A L
K   H   P   E   E   E   O
    L O U D H A I L E R
A   V   S   G   U   L   I
P L A N T A I N   D I D O
E   S   E   N   N   U
S T E E R A G E   A G E S
```

120

```
B R A I N W A V E   S   S
  O   N   I   I   E T A L
B O O T B L A C K   A   E
  K   O   F   T   O G L E
S   S   P U P I L   E   P
C Y M B A L   M I L D E W
A   A   G       V   I   A
P U L S A R   W E E V I L
E   L   N A D I R   E   K
G O T H   P   S   S   G
O   A   S P A D E W O R K
A B L Y   E   O   A   I
T   K   P R I M E T I M E
```

121

	C	H	O	I	C	E		C	A	D	E	T
	H	N		R		R		A		A		Y
P	E	D	A	L	O		J	A	G	U	A	R
	E	R		W		F		P		A		A
E	R	G	O		S	W	I	T	C	H	O	N
	U	L		N		T		I		I		T
	P	O	L	L	E	N	C	O	U	N	T	
C		W		S		H		M		R		
H	O	N	E	S	T	L	Y		B	A	I	L
I		G		H		F		R		D		
S	T	O	L	I	D		E	R	A	S	E	R
E		A		N		E		G			N	
L	O	L	L	Y		S	T	R	E	E	T	

122

W	H	I	S	K	E	R	S		G	R	O	W
A		N		I		E		R		A		O
T	A	K	E	N		S	H	U	T	T	E	R
T		L		G		U		L		E		R
	M	I	D	S	U	M	M	E	R	D	A	Y
E		N		L		E		S				I
N	U	G	G	E	T		C	O	M	M	O	N
C			Y		A		F		O			G
I	N	F	L	A	M	M	A	T	O	R	Y	
R		I		M		U		H		O		S
C	O	R	D	I	A	L		U	N	C	L	E
L		E		S		E		M		C		E
E	N	D	S		S	T	U	B	B	O	R	N

123

		S		S		M		F				
	R	A	C	E	M	E	E	T	I	N	G	
	O		A		A		R		L		R	
C	L	A	N		S	A	R	D	I	N	I	A
	L				H		Y		P		Z	
P	E	R	P	L	E	X		D	I	Z	Z	Y
	R		E		R		E		N		L	
A	B	B	E	Y		A	N	T	O	N	Y	M
	L		K		Q		V				B	
L	I	G	A	T	U	R	E		J	E	E	P
	N		B		A		L		O		A	
D	O	O	R	K	N	O	C	K	E	R		
		O		E		P		E				

124

E	C	O	N	O	M	I	S	T		G		A
	O		E		A		O		E	R	I	N
S	W	E	E	T	T	A	L	K		A		C
	L		R		I		D		I	N	C	H
F	I		E	N	D	E	D		D			O
A	N	N	A	L	S		R	A	P	P	E	R
I		S		U			N		R			I
R	A	P	I	D	S		A	D	R	I	F	T
T		E		E	N	T	R	Y		X		E
R	A	C	Y		O		C		B		H	
A		T		M	O	T	H	E	A	T	E	N
D	O	O	M		Z		E		R		R	E
E		R		V	E	R	S	A	T	I	L	E

SOLUTIONS

125

```
D E C E N T   H I T M A N
E   I   O     T   O   I
L A T I N   A L A D D I N
U   A   E   L   E   I   E
G O D U T C H   I N L E T
E   E   E     A       Y
    L O N G R A N G E
    E   E       P   T
S   P U T T S   N E R D I S H
P   U   E   T   C   E   G   O
A   T   T     C   E   G   O
C O N V E N E   C D R O M
E   E   G       U   A   A
D O T A G E   A R A M I S
```

126

```
      P   C   E   C
  S O U T H D A K O T A
  Q   C   O   R   L   D
S U L K   C A T H O L I C
  A   I   H   N   M
E S S E N C E   R I D E R
  H   U   E   M   S   A
S C O P E   F A G E N D S
  O   H   D   I       O
T U T O R I A L   F I Z Z
  R   R   X   B   L   E
  T R I N I D A D I A N
      A   E   G   P
```

127

```
    B   F   M     T
  B U R K I N A F A S O
  O   A   L   R   B   L
A G O G   B U R G U N D Y
  N   E   Y   L   K
C O M F O R T   B A K E D
  R   R   T   D   T   N
C R E A M   L I B E R T Y
  E   C   S   S       R
A G I T A T O R   L O O K
  I   U   I   O   E   A
S P R I N G B O A R D
    E   K   F   K
```

128

```
W I T H D R A W   F L A G
I   O   R     T   D   E   A
C A P R I   T W I S T E D
K   D   N   E   S   U   G
  C O O K I N G A P P L E
S   W   D   D   P       T
T E N U R E   S P I D E R
A   I   O   O   I   Y
I R R E V E R S I B L E
D   E   I   D   N   E   O
E N H A N C E   T I M I D
S   A   G   A   E   M   D
T U B A   G L A D R A G S
```

129

130

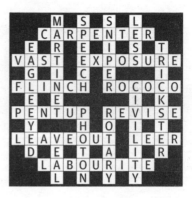

131

132

SOLUTIONS

133

```
    B B B D
  M A L A D R O I T
 D C   R   U   S   P
F E A T   R A I L C A R D
 T   E   O   S       E
B O R R O W   E U N U C H
 N   I           I   I
P A P A Y A   A U G U S T
 T     S   B   G   E
B O O K C L U B   L O L L
 R   I   E   E   I   Y
    N C E S S A N T
     D   P   S   G
```

134

```
A C R O B A T   B   F   S
F   E   R   E A R N E S T
T A P I O C A   E   I   O
E   L K   S P A N N E R E
R O Y C E   E   K   T   E
  U     N E R V O U S L Y
  S     H       N   U
S T E V E D O R E   N
P   D   A   R   S O G G Y
L O W B R O W   B   R   I
A   A   T   E M A N A T E
S U R R E A L   C   I   L
H   D   D   L I K E N E D
```

135

```
    C H E E S E D O F F
C   U   V   H   E   L
R E P L E T E   B L A S T
A   P   R   R   O   T   I
N O A H   F R E N E T I C
K   D   Y   A   O   K
S U B W A Y   W I M P L E
H   R   V   V   R   T
A N A L Y S I S   I F F Y
F   V   L   G   S   I   B
T I A R A   O N T A R I O
  D   M   U   Y   E   O
  O P P E R H E A D
```

136

```
H Y M N   S W I M W E A R
O   A   T   E   O   M   I
M I C R O B E   D E B U T
E   O   U   K   E   A   E
P A N I C   I M M U R E
A   H   N           G   I
G O O D Y T W O S H O E S
E   D       E   O       L
  A D M I R E   L L A M A
C   B   O   K   A   P   N
A G A I N   O R C H A R D
L   L   I   U   E   C   E
F E L I C I T Y   P E A R
```

137

```
P A R A P H E R N A L I A
L   S   A   O   N   T
S T O P   P E D I G R E E
R   I   P   I   E   M
F U N C T I O N A L
I   L   I       I   T
O S P R E Y   C O C C Y X
M   H       A       P
    I N D I S C R E E T
T   Z   E   T   U   C
C O L O R A D O   L E A K
D   M   L   F   E   S
M O M E N T O F T R U T H
```

138

```
H O B S O N S C H O I C E
I   U   N   Q   A   N   S
T O R   T O U R N E D O S
C   Y   H   I   G   E   A
H O S T E L R Y   S T A Y
    T   S   E   N   E   E
M E E K L Y   H O R R I D
I   D   Y   C   N   M
N U M B   H A S S L I N G
I   U   T   S   E   N   R
C O N D I T I O N   A M I
A   D   E   N   S   T   E
B E S I D E O N E S E L F
```

139

```
S L A P A N D T I C K L E
O   I   U   O   H   I
F I N E   M A L D E M E R
T   C   E   E   D   S
C E L E B R A T E D
R   A       A   M
R E N T A L   S E R M O N
D   E   T       L
    L E A D A S T R A Y
C   L   N   U   H   S
T O B O G G A N   R O S Y
O   F   E   C   O   E
A L L F O R T H E B E S T
```

140

```
C R O S S E S T   S T I R
U   R   U   Y   E   I   E
S M A R M   M A X I M U M
P   T   M   B   T   E   E
  T I M E H O N O U R E D
E   O   R   L   R   I
V A N I S H   S T O D G E
I   C   U   I   S
C L O T H E S H O R S E
T   P   O   E   N   E   F
I C E C O L D   A M A Z E
O   N   L   U   T   S   T
N O S Y   E P H E M E R A
```

SOLUTIONS

141

N	A	M	I	B	I	A		Q		M		S
E		E		E		C	O	U	R	A	G	E
C	L	A	U	D	I	A		E		S		N
K		N		S		D	E	E	P	S	E	T
S	U	S	H	I		I		N		I		R
	N			D	R	A	G	O	N	F	L	Y
	D		E			F				I		
H	O	M	E	M	A	T	C	H		E		
O		E		A		A		E	N	N	U	I
R	E	T	I	N	A	L		A		O		N
A		T		N		K	A	R	A	O	K	E
C	O	L	L	E	G	E		T		S		P
E		E		R		D	I	S	S	E	C	T

142

H	O	L	L	Y	H	O	C	K		D		F
	P		A		E		L		H	E	R	A
D	E	S	M	O	I	N	E	S		L		C
	N		P		F		V		A	I	M	S
G		A		M	E	L	E	E		C		I
R	A	P	T	O	R		R	A	D	I	U	M
A		P		U		G		O		I		
P	A	R	E	N	T		S	E	Q	U	E	L
E		E		T	A	P	I	R	S		S	E
S	O	H	O		B		T		G	K		
H		E		M	A	S	C	U	L	I	N	E
O	I	N	K		R		O		U		I	
T		D		A	D	A	M	S	M	I	T	H

143

W	R	I	T	L	A	R	G	E		O		P
	I		E		C		R		F	U	L	L
C	L	I	N	I	C	I	A	N		T		A
	L		D		O		M		B	O	S	S
A		E		C	R	A	M	P		F		T
C	A	N	A	R	D			Y	A	R	D	I	E
T		C		O				Y		A		R
S	C	H	U	S	S		S	U	B	T	L	E
O		A		S	T	E	E	P		E		D
F	U	N	K		O		R		S	B		
G		T		O	L	F	A	C	T	O	R	Y
O	P	E	N		E		P		E	A		
D		D		I	N	T	H	E	P	I	N	K

144

S	E	L	E	C	T		L	O	G	G	E	R
E		L		A		S		N		R		O
S	W	A	L	L	O	W		S	N	A	R	L
A		M		L		E		E		D		L
M	I	A	M	I		E	N	T	H	U	S	E
E				N		T				A		R
	D	O	G	G	Y	P	A	D	D	L	E	
I		F		O		O		O				F
S	A	F	E	B	E	T		O	D	D	E	R
R		H		I		A		R		R		I
A	G	A	I	N		T	E	D	D	I	E	S
E		N		G		O		I		L		K
L	E	D	G	E	R		R	E	A	L	L	Y

145

146

147

148

SOLUTIONS

149

150

151

152

153

```
E N V . . . I D A C T I C
S . E . . C . S . O . . E
P A G E . O A S T F U L
R . E . P . N . I . F . L
E N T H U S I A S M
S . A . F . C . T . M . D
S E T O F F . G A Z E B O
O . E . P . T . N . M . G
. . C A P R I C I O U S
F . P . S . I . E . R . B
I N A C T I V E . M I S O
N . N . R . I . . . A . D
D O G G Y B A G . P L O Y
```

154

```
S O U T H E N D O N S E A
A . P . E . U . P . T . P
D E S I R E D . E L I Z A
. . T . B . I . R . N . R
C L A M . S T R A I G H T
A . R . R . Y . B . . . M
L E T T E R . C L O C H E
L . . . T . F . E . H . N
E C S T A T I C . M I S T
D . L . I . N . S . A
O N I O N . I N N I N G S
F . N . E . S . U . T . A
F I G U R E H U G G I N G
```

155

```
. . B . M . F . A
. A R G Y B A R G Y
. P . E . F . V . O . G
S I F T . O P E N G O A L
. L . H . O . L . . . L
F L O R E T . A R G Y L E
. A . E . . . O . A
P R O N T O . C O R O N A
. B . . X . O . M . T
Y O U T H F U L . L I R A
. X . A . O . U . E . Y
. . E X T R E M I S T
. . I . D . N . S
```

156

```
H A S T H E H O T S F O R
O . E . U . A . E . A . E
D O N E G A L . N A K E D
. . A . O . T . D . E . P
B A T H . C E R E B R A L
E . O . H . D . R . . . A
F O R M A L . B E R G E N
U . . . C . G . D . R . E
D I S L I K E S . P A N T
D . I . E . I . F . P
L I N E N . S C R U P L E
E . U . D . H . E . L . A
D I S P A R A G E M E N T
```

SOLUTIONS

157

		W	S	A	J			
	C	O	R	N	F	L	O	U	R
P		O	A	W	R	S			
A	R	I	D	T	E	A	R	A	W	A	Y
O	W		C	Y		C			
I	M	P	I	S	H	S	O	M	B	R	E
I	N			A		I			
O	N	E	D	G	E	P	U	R	I	F	Y
E		D	A		Y	I			
I	N	A	C	T	I	O	N	R	A	C	E
T	R	S	A	O		E			
H	I	T	O	R	M	I	S	S			
B	N	A	E						

158

S	T	A	R	D	O	M	B	B	R
I	M	R	U	N	L	O	O	S	E
K	I	B	B	U	T	Z	O	D	D
H	L	M	Z	I	T	H	E	R	S
S	T	E	A	M	L	T	G	E
A	L	A	M	E	R	I	C	A	N	A
L	J	N	I
S	C	H	O	O	L	B	A	G	C
E	O	R	O	P	O	S	E	R
S	U	N	B	E	A	M	A	P	A
A	O	T	B	A	P	T	I	S	T
M	O	U	N	T	I	E	E	L	T
E	R	E	R	U	R	A	L	L	Y

159

H	A	M	F	I	S	T	E	D	D	I
N	O	U	F	V	E	I	N
S	T	I	L	L	L	I	F	E	M	T
E	K	L	O	W	I	D	E
P	S	P	E	E	R	S	T	R
O	B	T	A	I	N	T	H	R	A	L	L
U	A	X	O	S	U
N	U	T	M	E	G	C	E	A	S	E	D
D	U	L	A	G	O	S	E	E
S	E	E	K	L	B	N	D
I	T	T	O	U	R	N	E	D	O	S
G	U	T	S	R	A	O	M
N	E	P	E	R	S	O	N	N	E	L

160

G	O	T	H	I	C	N	O	V	E	L
F	F	A	H	W	X	C
A	F	F	E	C	T	I	O	N	E	G	O
S	K	R	E	C	W
H	A	M	A	S	P	E	R	T	U	R	B
I	A	A	Y	T	O
O	T	T	A	W	A	B	R	A	I	N	Y
N	R	M	E	V	B
S	H	I	H	T	Z	U	C	R	E	D	O
H	A	I	M	U	O
O	A	R	C	Y	B	E	R	N	A	U	T
W	C	K	A	V	G	S
C	H	E	S	H	I	R	E	C	A	T

161

162

163

164

SOLUTIONS

165

166

167

168

169

```
  N E W F O U N D L A N D
T M L   P   I   R   R
H I P P O   S I A M E S E
E   T   E   H   G   A   S
M A I M   C O L O S S U S
O   E   S   T   N       I
U N R U L Y   C A N C A N
S     U   L   L   O   G
E A R L G R E Y   F U N D
T   O   G   S   F   P   O
R A B B I T S   I N L A W
A   O   S   O   A   E   N
P I T C H A N D T O S S
```

170

```
S T E A D F A S T   B   G
  Y   H   O   E   F A I R
A P I A R I S T S   N   E
  O   B   L   O   O D I N
E   I   L E A F Y   I   A
N O G O O D   F O R C E D
I   N   U     K   O   I
G H O S T S   R E M O T E
M   R   S P O O L   T   R
A J A X   O   T   C   M
T   N   D I R T C H E A P
I N C H   L   E   I   R
C   E   O S T R A C I S M
```

171

```
H A B I T A T   H   T   L
Y   A   I   I R O N O R E
D E C A M P S   T   B   S
R   K   E   S C H L O S S
A T S E A   U   E   O   E
  O   F R E M A N T L E
  G   T   D     I
C O O P E R A T E   N
R   P   R   I   D E P O T
A S T U T E R   N   O   I
B   O   I   B R E A K I N
B R U M M I E S   E   G
Y   T   E   D E S E R V E
```

172

```
    A N C H O R A G E
A   B   V   U   I   D   A
N O I S E   B O L I V A R
D   O   M   B   Y   A   S
N O G O A R E A   S N I P
O   R   R   D   T   T   L
M E A N I E   S A L A M I
I   P   A   D   L   G   T
S O H O   P E N I T E N T
T   I   Z   C   S   O   I
A R C H I V E   M O U R N
K   A   N   I   A   S   G
E N L I G H T E N
```

SOLUTIONS

173

```
  N U T S A N D B O L T S
W   P O   E   A   O     A
H U R R Y   A I R P O R T
E   I   A   T   B   S   I
E D G E   R E F E R E E S
L   H   T   N   C       F
B U T T O N   R U S S I A
A       M   V   E   Q   C
R E S T O R E D   A U N T
R   A   R   N   S   E   O
O F F E R E D   C L E A R
W   E   O   E   A   Z   Y
S T R A W B E R R I E S
```

174

```
B A R N   S T I C K L E R
I   E       E   A   O   U
D U T Y   C A R P E T E D
D   I   A   U   I   H   E
A C C E L E R A T E
B   E   L   N   U   A   S
L E N G T H   A L I G H T
E   T   H   V   A   I   U
    D E V A S T A T E D
F   S   R   S   E   P   I
A P P R A I S E   T R I O
N   U   G   A       O   U
G I N G E R L Y   O P U S
```

175

```
  A F G H A N I S T A N
A   E   O   A   H   N   B
T R E A S U R E R   I R E
T   T   R   E   M   L
H A L V E   O D D B A L L
E   I   S   W   T   I
D I G E S T   I D L I N G
O   H   A   I   O   E
U N T A M E D   O W N E R
B   S   U   M   C   E
L E O   R A I S E C A I N
E   U   A   R   S   C   T
  A T A L L E V E N T S
```

176

```
  C A N A D A G O O S E
C   P   C   P   N   O   C
H Y P N O T I S T   B R A
I   L   A   A   R   P
C O C K Y   R E P T I L E
K   A   T   Y   Q   K
E N V I E D   M O D U L E
N   A   S   R   E   N
K I L L J O Y   B A T O N
I   C   U   R   I   E
E R A   D R I F T W O O D
V   D   A   A   U   Y
P E R S O N A L I T Y
```

177

```
  P O S T H U M O U S
  L   M   A   A   S   P
T A X A T I O N   U N I T
  C   S   L   I   R   E
  E C H O   S C E P T R E
      U   H   U       C
  A P P R O P R I A T E
  I   L     E   S
P R E C E D E   C H I P
  W   O   B   D   A   O
D A R N   A L A R M I S T
  Y   G   C   D   E   E
  B A C K H A N D E R
```

178

```
    C O L D C A L L E R
R   R   U   O   A   X
U N A I D E D   M O P E D
N   T   O D   E   I   E
A B E L   G L A D R A G S
G     P   E   U   T   C
R E P O R T   A C C E D E
O   U   U   L   K       N
U L T E R I O R   P L O D
N   D   I   U   O   I   I
D R O N E   V E N I S O N
    W   N   R   C   Z   G
  A N D T H E R E S T
```

179

```
R E B U K E   T A L C U M
E   A   O   B   D   O   A
A R R A N G E   I A M B I
S   G   T   N   E   P   M
O B E L I   G L U C O S E
N       K   A       T   D
  C H A I N L E T T E R
A   U       T   Y       F
Z A M B E Z I   P E A R L
O   B   G   G   H   R   A
R A L L Y   E T O N I A N
E   E   P   R   O   S   G
S P R I T E   A N N E X E
```

180

```
F A T E   B A R B I C A N
U   I   R   T   O   H   E
G O N D O L A   S H A K E
I   E   D   S   O   T   D
T R A D E   T O M A T O
I       N   A       E   D
V A U L T I N G H O R S E
E   N       D   A       F
  S T A M P S   R I N S E
C   A   A   T   O   A   A
H U M A N   I L L I C I T
A   E   I   L   D   H   E
R I D I C U L E   F O R D
```

SOLUTIONS

181

182

183

184

185

```
    A N A L G E S I C
S M B   M   A   T   O
O S A K A   B E L G I A N
U D   T   L   L   C   T
T R E A T I E S   S K Y E
H   M   O   S   T   Y M
P H O B I A   B R E W U P
A   I   R   N   I   I L
C O S Y   L A M A N C H A
I   E   P   U   N   K T
F I L L I E S   G E E S E
I   L   N   E   L   T D
C H E C K M A T E
```

186

```
P R A C T I C A L J O K E
O   N   H   A   I   T   P
P I G T A I L   N O T C H
    U   W   L   G   E   E
P U L L   T E L E G R A M
I   A   B   D   R       E
K E R N E L   M I R R O R
E       R   C   E   A   A
S U N V I S O R   E V I L
T   A   B   C   T   I
A D D L E   O M I N O U S
F   I   R   O   F   L   U
F O R E I G N O F F I C E
```

187

```
  C R O S S P A T C H
A   O X   U   V   H
B U R G E O N   I S A A C
O   A   N   D   A   M   O
V I L E   H E I R L O O M
E       C   W   I   I   M
B Y W A Y S   G E I S H A
O   E   R   S   S       N
A L L R I G H T   A C I D
R   C   L   U   J   O   E
D R O L L   T R A I P S E
    M   I   U   D   I   R
P E R C I P I E N T
```

188

```
      F   S   S   M
    H A R L E Q U I N
  B   C   O   U   L   A
C O P T   W H I S K E R Y
  O   O   E   R       A
S K A T E R   T R I L B Y
  M   U           R   E
G A M M O N   C U R T S Y
  K   A   U   I   Q
D E V O U R E D   T A U T
  R   B   R   D   A   E
  D E C O L L E T E
      Y   W   E   E
```

189

190

191

192

193

Grid 193 — across/down answers: HARDCHEESE, FULCRUM, ALLOW, EYOT, INVITING, SIMIAN, DENTAL, ALLCLEAR, BLUR, EXTRA, GROUCHO, HANKYPANKY

194

Grid 194 — answers: POWERSTEERING, EARNEST, ROWAN, ACME, LAIDINTO, TINTIN, SCORED, GEOMETRY, USER, ALIBI, ABUSING, HALFHEARTEDLY

195

Grid 195 — answers: DILETTANTE, PERCENT, NORTH, EURO, VUVUZELA, LIMPID, SCYTHE, MONTEREY, EBBS, TWEET, VERSION, BUFFERZONE

196

Grid 196 — answers: COFFEESHOPS, HITANDRUN, SET, RECUR, CLEANER, STABLE, BISTRO, ATELIER, HILLY, IRE, INNERTUBE, UNIMPORTANT

SOLUTIONS

197

D	E	A	D	A	N	D	B	U	R	I	E	D
	L		R		O		A		A		Y	
Z	E	R	O		V	I	L	I	F	I	E	D
	C		O		I		T		T		S	
S	T	A	L	A	C	T	I	T	E			
	R		M		E				R		S	
H	O	L	M	E	S		B	A	S	I	C	S
	N		O				I				H	
		N	I	G	H	T	M	A	R	E	S	
	B		O		R		T		M		D	
C	O	N	C	E	I	V	E		P	L	U	G
	E		L		E		R		L		L	
G	R	E	E	N	F	I	N	G	E	R	E	D

198

P	A	R	T	Y	P	O	L	I	T	I	C	S
	I		E		U		I		R		H	
T	R	E	E		C	O	N	F	U	S	E	D
	R		T		K		E		N		F	
H	I	G	H	M	I	N	D	E	D			
	F				S				L		B	
G	L	I	T	C	H		B	L	E	A	R	Y
	E		O				I				E	
			A	N	T	I	F	R	E	E	Z	E
	A		S		O		O		N		H	
P	L	A	T	O	N	I	C		R	U	N	G
	G		I		G		A		O		E	
B	A	S	E	B	A	L	L	G	L	O	V	E

199

	C	H	A	M	B	E	R	L	A	I	N	
S		E		O		M		U		M		P
Y	O	M	K	I	P	P	U	R		P	A	L
N			S		L		I		A			A
C	A	B	O	T		O	R	D	E	R	L	Y
H		A		E		Y			T			F
R	E	L	E	N	T		L	I	B	I	D	O
O		A		D		C		A				R
N	U	C	L	E	A	R		E	C	L	A	T
O		L		M		O		B				I
U	S	A		E	U	P	H	E	M	I	S	M
S		V		N		I		R		D		E
	L	A	N	D	I	N	G	G	E	A	R	

200

B	U	T	T	E	R	F	I	N	G	E	R	S
I		A		A		E		O		N		T
D	I	V	E	R	S	E		T	E	N	O	R
	E		N		L		E		U			I
N	O	R	M		R	E	D	B	R	I	C	K
O		N		D		R		O				E
T	R	A	G	I	C		V	O	X	P	O	P
O				S		U		K		A		A
R	E	T	I	R	I	N	G		O	R	G	Y
I		W		A		P		E		Q		
O	L	I	V	E		L	A	W	S	U	I	T
U		S		L		U		E		E		O
S	I	T	T	I	N	G	P	R	E	T	T	Y

201

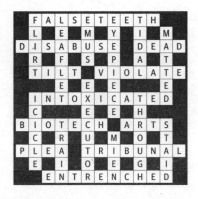

202

203

204

SOLUTIONS

205

206

207

208

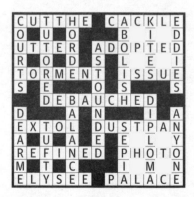

209

J E R R Y L E E L E W I S
U O · A · N · O · A · · E
N I T · C A S S O U L E T
T T H · U · T · T · · · T
A P E R T U R E · W E L L
· · N · I · E · R · R · E
R U B E N S · W E I M A R
A · O · G · D · P · A · ·
P E R U · C O H O S T E D
I · O · W · M · R · T · A
E X U B E R A N T · H E N
R · G · L · I · E · A · T
S C H A D E N F R E U D E

210

F A C A D E · U P H O L D
I · O · I · · O · P · E
E X U L T · D I T T I E S
R · L · C · I · S · U · I
C L O T H E S · H O M E R
E · M · P · O · · · E
· B E E F E A T E R ·
S · M · R · · E · P
H A R E M · S T A M M E R
U · E · Y · E · R · O · O
T I C K L E D · G I V E N
U · U · O · · O · E · G
P O R O U S · A N O D E S

211

S C R A P E D · E · E · T
O · · R · R O M A N C E
L U L L A B Y · B · T · N
F E W · I R A N I A N
A P R O N · C · R · R · I
· I · · C H E E R L E S S
· K · O · · A · · N
S E A S C A P E S · A
K · C · K · · S Y L P H
E R R A T I C · M · A · O
T · O · A · K N E E S U P
C A S T I L E · N · S · I
H · S · L · D E T R O I T

212

P O N T I U S P I L A T E
R · E · T · A · N · I · I
O U T S E L L · F L O O D
· · B · M · M · U · L · E
S H A M · C O S T L I E R
W · L · O · N · U · · · D
I N L A N D · B R A N D O
T · · T · A · E · E · W
C A P E H O R N · S W A N
H · R · E · C · B · M
O D O U R · T R E F O I L
F · W · U · I · E · O · O
F I L I N G C A B I N E T

SOLUTIONS

213

214

215

216

217

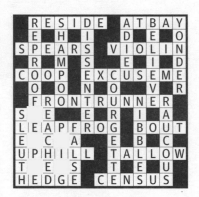

```
V A L U A B L E _ T R O T
A _ E _ D _ O _ F _ H _ U
S A V E D _ U N I C O R N
T _ E _ I _ C _ D _ N _ G
_ W R E T C H E D N E S S
A _ E _ I _ E _ L _ _ T
R E D H O T _ N E E D L E
K _ _ N _ A _ F _ E _ N
A C Q U A I N T A N C E _
N _ U _ L _ S _ D _ R _ I
S W A L L O W _ D E E D S
A _ R _ Y _ E _ L _ E _ P
S E T T _ F R I E N D L Y
```

218

```
_ P I R A T E _ T U M I D
_ I _ E _ O _ R _ O _ I
R E C A L L _ C A N N O N
_ B _ D _ E _ D _ A _ G
S A R I _ R E F E R R A L
_ L _ L _ A _ A _ _ C _ E
_ D A Y A N D N I G H T _ T
S _ D _ C _ C _ E _ R
T R I C K E R Y _ N A I L
U _ P _ I _ F _ T _ C
C H O I C E _ R O L L E R
C _ S _ K _ E _ E _ P
O P E N S _ V E R S U S
```

219

```
_ R E S I D E _ A T B A Y
E _ H _ I _ D _ E _ O
S P E A R S _ V I O L I N
_ R _ M _ S _ E _ I _ D
C O O P _ E X C U S E M E
O _ O _ N _ O _ V _ R
_ F R O N T R U N N E R
S _ E _ E _ R _ I _ A
L E A P F R O G _ B O U T
E _ C _ A _ E _ B _ C
U P H I L L _ T A L L O W
T _ E _ S _ T _ E _ U
H E D G E _ C E N S U S
```

220

```
_ _ C O M P A S S I O N
G _ R _ O _ T _ E _ R
O P E N O U T _ R I V E R
T _ M _ R _ I _ A _ I _ O
O V A L _ P R O P H E S Y
P _ _ F _ E _ H _ T _ O
I N F I R M _ R I G O U R
E _ U _ A _ P _ C _ _ B
C A R O U S A L _ K E P I
E _ I _ L _ E _ A _ X _ S
S P O D E _ L U M B A G O
_ S _ I _ L _ M _ L _ N
R O U N D A B O U T
```

SOLUTIONS

221

```
 O R C H E S T R A T E D
T U   I   A   E   O   I
R I S E R   P I V O T A L
A   T   E   P   I   E   A
N I L E   M E S S E D U P
S   E   C   R   I   P
F U R R O W   V O I C E D
I   M   S   N   E   A
G R I P P I N G   F R E T
U   D   L   E   R   T   I
R E L E A S E   I M A G O
E   E   I   Z   F   I   N
D I S I N F E C T A N T
```

222

```
J A L O P Y   S M A L L S
E   A   E     O   O   W
T A P A S   C O N F U S E
L   W   T   H   T   I   A
A R I Z O N A   A S S E T
G   N       M   N       Y
    G A N G P L A N K
S       A   A       N   J
T I G H T   G O N D O L A
R   I   U   N   A   C   U
O B V E R S E   T O K E N
N   E   A       A   E   T
G A R G L E   S L U R R Y
```

223

```
 S H U T T L E C O C K
S U   R   E   H   E   G
N U M B E R T W O   L I E
O       K   O   U   L   T
W H A C K   F O X H U N T
G   N   E   F       L   O
O X C A R T   O B L O N G
G   I   C   L   S   E
G A L U M P H   E V E R T
L   L   I   A   M       H
E R A   M U L T I T U D E
S   R   I   E   S   R   R
  E Y E C A T C H I N G
```

224

```
  P E C C A D I L L O
S L   U   F   M   E
T O O L B A R   P S A L M
U   N   E   A   R   T   O
P O K E   R I C O C H E T
E   E   D   P   E   O
N I C E T Y   T E R R O R
D   A   H   H   R       C
O U T S I D E R   U G L Y
U   H   O   C   T   L   C
S C O O P   T U R M O I L
E   D   I   I   U   R   E
D E B A U C H E R Y
```